NASCAR NOW!

SECOND EDITION

**TIMOTHY MILLER
& STEVE MILTON**

FIREFLY BOOKS

A FIREFLY BOOK

Published by Firefly Books Ltd. 2006

First printing

Publisher Cataloging-in-Publication Data (U.S.)
Miller, Timothy, 1951-
  NASCAR now! / by Timothy Miller and Steve Milton.
  2nd ed.
[176] p. : col. photos. ; cm.
Summary: Guide to NASCAR and stock car racing;
including biographies of drivers, analysis of racing teams,
history of stock car racing and famous track venues.
ISBN-13: 978-1-55407-148-7(pbk.)
ISBN-10: 1-55407-148-8 (pbk.)
1. NASCAR (Association).
2. Stock car racing – United States.
3. Automobile racing drivers – United States.
I. Milton, Steve. II. Title.
796.72/0973 dc22   GV1029.9 S74M56 2006

**Library and Archives Canada Cataloguing
in Publication**
Miller, Timothy, 1951-
  NASCAR now! / Timothy Miller and Steve Milton.
  – 2nd ed.
ISBN-13: 978-1-55407-148-7
ISBN-10: 1-55407-148-8
1. NASCAR (Association).
2. Stock car racing – United States.
3. Automobile racing drivers – United States.
I. Milton, Steve II. Title.
GV1029.9.S74M54 2006 796.720973 C2006-901672-0

Published in the United States by
Firefly Books (U.S.) Inc.
P.O. Box 1338, Ellicott Station
Buffalo, New York 14205

Published in Canada by
Firefly Books Ltd.
66 Leek Crescent
Richmond Hill, Ontario L4B 1H1

Cover and interior design by Gareth Lind / LINDdesign

Printed in Canada

The publisher gratefully acknowledges the financial
support for our publishing program by the Government
of Canada through the Book Publishing Industry
Development Program.

Statistics include all races through the 2005 season.

CONTENTS

INTRODUCTION

The essence of NASCAR. Jimmie Johnson (48) crosses the finish line in front of second place Matt Kenseth (17) to win the UAW-DaimlerChrysler 400 at Las Vegas Motor Speedway, March 12, 2006.

NASCAR is a sport. NASCAR is entertainment. And NASCAR is a cultural phenomenon.

From humble beginnings in races on the beaches in Florida and the dusty dirt tracks south of the Mason-Dixon Line, NASCAR stock car racing has exploded to the forefront of the sporting and cultural worlds, surpassing older sports in attendance and media attention. And through solid and insightful business practices, NASCAR has succeeded beyond all expectation as a financial giant.

NASCAR's main appeal is that its relatively simple racing machines resemble everyday cars fans can relate to. And the stars of NASCAR, the drivers, are approachable athletes who are

not above putting back into the sport what they reap from it. Cup drivers are revered as folk heroes, and some have become national idols as part of the fabric of society. Driver rivalries are intense, and the competition between auto manufacturers is fierce.

Every weekend hundreds of thousands of fans – and millions more watching on television – witness the color, the noise and the excitement as dozens of sleek race cars and compelling drivers provide heart-stopping action in a competition like no other.

Over six million people attend NASCAR Nextel Cup races annually, with an estimated 275 million viewing the races on national broadcasts around the globe. The 36 separate

Nextel Cup events average 186,000 spectators. One Cup race draws more fans than the Super Bowl, a World Series Baseball game and a National League Basketball finals game combined. Billions of dollars are invested in sponsorship and promotion, and licensed NASCAR merchandise tops $2 billion per year.

NASCAR races are unique. Each race stands on its own as a major event with its own sense of urgency and importance, not unlike a playoff game in another sport. And there is only one Cup race per week.

NASCAR's stock car racing has grown to unprecedented levels since Bill France's original vision back in 1949. His hard work and sound business acumen have been continued through the efforts of his son, Bill Jr., and now grandson Brian.

NASCAR Now! covers the entire spectrum of this phenomenon. Along with the history of the sport, you'll read about some of the colorful personalities who helped make NASCAR what it is today. You'll pick up the latest in safety technology and learn more about the tracks and how the drivers win points. You'll discover the action and function of pit stops, meet the hottest and most influential drivers of today's NASCAR scene, get some first-hand, behind-the-scenes interviews and take a look at the marketing machine that fuels the sport.

So get buckled up and press that starter. It's time for the green flag.

Jimmie Johnson, winner of the 2006 Daytona 500, is all smiles after winning the first and biggest Cup race of the season. He won over $1.5 million. By contrast, Lee Petty, winner of the inaugural Daytona 500 in 1959, took home $19,050.

Curtis Turner and his Ford convertible at Daytona Beach. The soft-top division ran for several years in the late 1950s.

The real roots of stock car racing go back about 100 years to the introduction of the automobile.

Motoring contests were held in Europe and North America during the automobile's formative years, but the contests were quite different in makeup on each side of the Atlantic Ocean.

European and British racing was performed on local roads and thoroughfares, evolving into road racing. Spectators lined streets and country roads as the cars roared past them only feet away. Eventually this road racing was curtailed with the advent of specially designed and constructed circuits that continue to this day.

In North America, road racing was the mainstay of early competition, but automobiles were expensive, and those who raced were usually wealthy sportsmen. By 1910, with the help of Ford's Model T, automobiles were more affordable to the masses and anyone with a competitive spirit could go racing.

But where to race? Aside from populated areas in the eastern United States, most roads were nothing more than wagon paths, and extensive auto travel was virtually impossible. So races were held at county fairgrounds, where there were already nice, smooth, oval-shaped horse-racing tracks.

By World War I, racing on these mostly dirt ovals had become very popular. Carl Fisher's 2.5-mile brick-paved oval just outside of Indianapolis, built in 1909 (now Indianapolis Motor Speedway), took racing to new levels.

A multitude of wood-surfaced board tracks, a successor to bicycle velodromes, were constructed around the country over the next 20 years. Soon the cars that raced on the board and dirt tracks became pure racing machines. At first the cars were basically larger automobiles such as Mercedes-Benz, Hudson or Stutz roadsters with the fenders removed. By 1930 the forerunners of today's Indy-style car, the Duesenberg and Miller, dominated American racing.

While the Indy-style roadster developed through the 1930s – benefiting from national sanctioning by the Contest Board of the American Automobile Association (AAA) – smaller versions of these cars, including Sprint and Midget cars, plied the local fairgrounds, especially in the Northeast and Midwest United States.

A movement was also taking place in the South. In an effort to outrun government agents with cars full of illegally made whiskey, "moonshine" runners were modifying stock street cars and becoming successful at delivering the goods. The car of choice was usually the light, nimble and fast V8-powered Ford.

Soon the moonshine runners wanted to pit their driving talents against each other, so informal contests started, usually on a hastily built dirt oval in a farm field. As these impromptu contests grew and became popular, family and friends would appear to watch the bragging rights. Bleachers were built, hot dogs sold and prize money awarded.

To the north, full-fendered stock car racing, known as "jalopy" or "Modified" racing, was a mainstay on the ovals along with the AAA Indy-type cars, but these "stock" cars were far from stock with their modified engines, suspensions and cut-down bodywork. The cars of the South were more stock-like in appearance.

At this time, there was no unity with all the racers and tracks. Each track had its own set of rules and car specs. There was no overall governing body like the AAA's Contest Board.

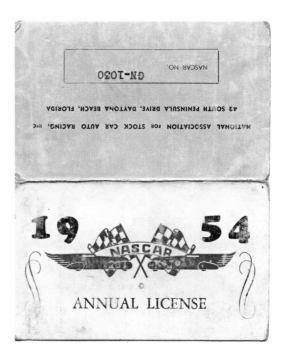

An early annual license, issued six years after NASCAR was legally incorporated. The holder of this card was a race car driver from Canada.

Enter Bill France. An auto mechanic from the Washington D.C. area, France moved to Daytona Beach on Florida's east coast in 1934 and set up shop. He raced his Modified in Florida and successfully promoted some small beach/road events at Daytona, but by the end of World War II he was thinking about a national sanctioning body that could oversee this type of racing. The AAA wasn't interested in racing cars that looked like anything you could drive off a car lot.

After meetings with other promoters, car owners and drivers just before Christmas of 1947, the foundations were laid, and in February 1948 the National Association for Stock Car Auto Racing (NASCAR) was legally incorporated.

For the first two years of its existence, NASCAR ran only a Modified class, but France believed if fans could identify with the cars on the tracks, they would bond with the sport. In 1949 France's vision and hard work came to life with NASCAR's new Strictly Stock division. Organized stock car racing was born.

The first race in this class was held in June 1949 at the new three-quarter mile Charlotte, North Carolina, dirt track (now Charlotte Speedway). With a purse of $2,000 and 13,000 fans to witness the event, this first race demonstrated that France meant business.

Daytona Beach in 1957, with a large crowd waiting for the race to begin. Lots of people, no stands, and no protection from a car careening into the crowd.

Although Glenn Dunnaway was the first to complete the 200-lap event, officials disqualified him as his Ford was running with illegal rear springs. So the first winner of a NASCAR stock car race was Jim Roper in his '49 Lincoln.

In 1950 the first NASCAR-based speedway opened – the 1.25-mile Darlington Raceway in South Carolina – with the first of many Southern 500 races.

In the early 1950s, NASCAR expanded from its southern roots to travel west to California and Arizona, and north to Michigan. The showroom stock cars became less and less showroom in appearance and performance, sporting the largest engines available, more safety equipment, and heavy-duty brakes and suspensions.

As the decade progressed, more racetracks were built – substantial facilities with seating and amenities approaching those of baseball parks. As the sport grew, newly built tracks were all paved.

Stock car racing reached a level of maturity in 1959 with the opening of the Daytona International Speedway. The brainchild of Bill France, this 2.5-mile-long oval with 31-degree corner banking was constructed on 480 acres of northern Florida land. The track was built to replace the 4.1-mile oval-shaped beach/road course that NASCAR ran on the Atlantic shore in February.

The vast vista of the Daytona oval left fans goggle-eyed, and the racers took to this new

track right away. Cotton Owens set the pace in a Pontiac, with a top qualifying speed of over 143 miles per hour. And in a photo finish that decided the inaugural Daytona 500 race victor some days later, Lee Petty, in a '59 Oldsmobile, was declared the winner over Johnny Beauchamp and his Thunderbird, who originally took the checkered flag.

Starting in the early 1960s, NASCAR acquired many new fans as some of its events were televised. The sport grew in popularity and professionalism, and it became big business with the involvement of corporate sponsorship. A new generation of drivers emerged. Car manufacturers built cars specifically with winning races in mind. Tire companies devoted personnel exclusively to race car research and development. While this expansion took place, Bill France ran NASCAR with a firm hand.

At this time, one driver more than any other allowed NASCAR to flourish, and that driver was Richard Petty. This dark-haired, lanky second-generation driver from North Carolina started his career in 1958, and became the undisputed "King" of stock car racing until his retirement in 1992. Many of his accomplishments will never be equaled. Some of his records include the most wins (200), most pole positions (127) and most consecutive wins (10 in 1967).

An immensely popular driver, Petty, with his series of Plymouths, became the sport's top ambassador. He spent almost as much time at the track signing autographs for his fans as he did behind the wheel. He is probably the most interviewed personality in any sport, and always gave back to the sport what he accomplished over his 35 years of racing.

In addition to NASCAR, another racing body was also involved in stock car racing during this time. When the AAA dropped its involvement with auto racing in 1955, the United States Auto Club (USAC) was formed, and it became the sanctioning body for most open-wheel racing, including Sprint, Midget and Champ (Indy) car events.

USAC also had a stock car series, and was prominent in areas other than the southern United States. Although the USAC stock car series did not race as often as NASCAR, it provided some fierce competition with a lot of "box office" drivers of the day – drivers who were well-known from racing the Champ cars at tracks such as Pocono, Milwaukee and, of course, Indy.

Some of the more prominent USAC competitors were household names. Drivers such as A.J. Foyt, Mario Andretti and Parnelli Jones all raced stock cars on the USAC circuit along with piloting the open-wheel Champ

Same race, seven years later. No more rooster tails in the sand now as the Fords, Pontiacs and Mercurys take to the 2.5-mile tri-oval for the Daytona 500.

Fights between drivers were not uncommon, but they were never before a live television audience when CBS broadcast the Daytona 500 in 1979. During the final stages of this race, the first to go before a national live audience, Donnie Allison (No. 1) and Cale Yarborough (No. 11) tussled on the final lap while Allison was in the lead, and both cars ended up parked on the infield. Words between the drivers were traded, and then punches as Donnie (left), and then his brother Bobby (with helmet on) tag-teamed on Yarborough (right). Just good ol' boys exchanging views, something that would not be tolerated today. By the way, Richard Petty won the race, the fight was a draw and a lot more people turned on their televisions for the next race.

cars. There were several stock-car-only drivers who could, and did, drive as well as anyone in NASCAR racing. Norm Nelson, Don White and Paul Goldsmith were just some of USAC's "regulars."

By 1970, however, there was a lot of internal strife at USAC, and its stock division fell by the wayside. While USAC continued with open-wheeled racing, the Indy-car series was taken over by Championship Auto Racing Teams (CART) in 1979. USAC is still a sanctioning body for Sprint and Midget competitions, as well as a dirt track Late Model Series.

In 1971, NASCAR entered what is considered its "modern" era. Tobacco giant R.J. Reynolds gave its financial support to NASCAR's top division, and the Winston Cup was born, a relationship that grew and prospered until 2003.

Also at this time, television started taking an active role in presenting Winston Cup races, starting with ABC's *Wide World of Sports* broadcasts. With this new exposure, large corporations such as Coca-Cola, Procter & Gamble and STP began to see the potential benefit of being financially involved in racing.

The first race to be televised live in its entirety was the Daytona 500 in 1979. An estimated 20 million viewers watched Petty win the 500 as late-race leaders Cale Yarborough and Bobby Allison collided on the last lap, got out of their cars and started fighting while Petty took the checkered flag. All of this race action and drama, on and off the track, unfolded in front of millions of viewers

and gave NASCAR a tremendous boost in popularity.

In the early 1980s, as Detroit began producing smaller, more fuel-efficient automobiles, NASCAR followed suit, and race cars were "downsized" with wheelbases of 110 inches for the new sedans. Also at this time, new drivers were making their mark in Winston Cup competition. The most prominent were Dale Earnhardt, Darrell Waltrip and Bill Elliott.

Earnhardt, a second-generation driver, was one of the sport's most controversial figures. He ran with a fearless intensity, and earned the name "The Intimidator." This North Carolina native also won the NASCAR championship seven times before his untimely racing death at the 2001 Daytona 500.

Waltrip, a brash newcomer from Tennessee, felt he could oust the veterans and was quite vocal about his plan. "Jaws" (as he was called early in his career) accomplished what he said he would, breaking the older drivers' monopoly on the sport by winning the title in 1981, 1982 and 1985. He raced until 1996 and is now one of the sport's broadcast personalities.

After a relatively slow start in racing in the late 1970s, Georgia's Bill Elliott would personify Winston Cup racing in the 1980s. He progressed through the ranks, winning the championship in 1988. Elliott earned fame by capturing the Winston Million – an award of $1 million for winning three of NASCAR's four biggest races. By winning the Daytona 500, the Winston 500 and the Southern 500 in 1985, Elliott became known as "Million Dollar Bill"

and "Awesome Bill from Dawsonville." Elliott continues to race in NASCAR's top division.

One of the most controversial changes in stock car racing at the NASCAR level took place in 1987. With the ever-increasing speeds, safety became an important issue, and NASCAR instituted "restrictor plates," a device between the race car engine's carburetor and intake manifold. This plate reduces the fuel/air mixture in the engine, reducing engine power, hence reducing car speed. These devices are mandatory on the larger superspeedways like Daytona and Talladega.

Other safety developments have been instituted in the past few years, including roof flaps to reduce the possibility of cars becoming airborne, pit road rules and reduced pit lane speeds, and crash-absorbing barrier walls.

NASCAR has also expanded its track horizons, replacing older, smaller tracks with new facilities such as Fontana and Texas to hold the legions of fans. Two road-racing circuits are now part of the 36-race schedule. Watkins Glen and Sears Point give Cup teams a new outlook on racing the traditional oval-track cars.

Growth in NASCAR took a big step forward in August 1994, when the first Cup race was held at the Indianapolis Motor Speedway, the first race ever to be run at Indy aside from the Indy 500 Memorial Day classic held since 1911. Winning the inaugural Brickyard 400 at Indy was a young Jeff Gordon, who would go on to capture the 1995 Winston Cup title.

Gordon is one of the new breed of NASCAR stars who continues to dominate the sport.

While older drivers such as Terry Labonte, Rusty Wallace and Ken Schrader continue to race, younger drivers such as Gordon, Matt Kenseth and Tony Stewart exemplify NASCAR's current driving superstars.

The biggest recent change to NASCAR came at the end of the 2003 season. After a 32-year relationship, tobacco giant R.J. Reynolds relinquished the title sponsorship of NASCAR's premier stock car series. The wireless technology company Nextel Communications, based in Reston, Virginia, then partnered with NASCAR in presenting the top series, now called the Nextel Cup. This is a 10-year deal that began at the start of the 2004 season.

With Nextel's involvement, NASCAR's top stock car series has acquired its fourth name. In 1949, NASCAR's first year, the stock car series was known as the Strictly Stock division, to differentiate it from the Modified and Roadster classes. In 1950 the stock class became known as the Grand National and remained the name of the top class until 1970.

In 1971, R.J. Reynolds (under its Winston brand) teamed up with NASCAR, and the races were known as the Winston Cup Grand National events until 1986 when the "Grand National" designation was dropped. NASCAR has kept the Grand National name for its feeder stock car series, combining the Busch North Series and the Winston West Series into one entity that is now known as the NASCAR Grand National.

NASCAR ABROAD

NASCAR ventured south into Mexico in 2005 for the first time. The Busch race was held at the Autodromo Hermanos Rodriguez Race Course in Mexico City.

NASCAR has rarely strayed from its U.S. roots. Early in its life, races were held in Canada, the United States' neighbor to the north.

During the past 10 years NASCAR has ventured into Japan and Mexico with events, but the Japanese races were Cup exhibition races and Busch Series races. Similarly, the Tercel-Motorola Mexico 200 was a Busch Series race held in March of 2005, and won by Martin Truex Jr.

Three exhibition races were held in Japan in 1996, including an event on the Suzuka road course won by Rusty Wallace. In 1997 Mike Skinner won at Suzuka, and he won again in 1998 on the Honda-built 1.5-mile Twin Ring

Motegi Oval. A NASCAR Winston West points race was held at Motegi in 1999, but since then the track has been the scene of CART and IRL events only.

As part of its Dodge Weekly Racing Series, NASCAR has a presence on a local level in Canada. But there have been two major NASCAR races in Canada. The first of these was held July 1, 1952, at Stamford Park in Niagara Falls on a half-mile dirt horse track.

The course hosted event 18 of the 34-race Grand National schedule, a 200-lapper on a track that had gained a reputation as being hard on race cars, with its flat rutted surface and board fences that could pierce through a car if broken. After two hours and 11 minutes,

Buddy Shuman of Charlotte, North Carolina, led the 17 others to victory in his 1952 Hudson Hornet. The track was so rough that only seven cars were running at the end as wheels and suspensions broke on the unforgiving surface.

Some drivers at Stamford Park who made the long trek from the southern United States would become icons in NASCAR racing. The Flock Brothers, Fonty and Tim, came from Atlanta. Fonty took seventh in his Henry J, while Tim, who started second, got in a smash-up and placed 13th in his Hudson. The engine in Lee Petty's Plymouth gave up after 40 laps, and the North Carolina native took 16th.

There was one Canadian in the field. Albert Lemieux of Montreal started the race 17th in his 1950 Meteor (the Canadian version of a Ford) and placed 10th.

Lee Petty was driving Oldsmobiles when he came to Canada for the country's second NASCAR GN race on the paved third-mile oval at Toronto's Canadian National Exhibition grounds on July 18, 1958. There were 19 cars for the 30th race of the 51-race schedule, a 100-lapper that was not well received by the fans, according to press reports of the day.

Petty won the race, but it seems his win was not as important as the regular weekly racing. "Lee Petty of Randleman, N.C., won the supposed high-light of last night's card – the 100-lap late model race," said a report in the *Toronto Star*. "A few minor collisions marred the running of the 100-lapper but nothing serious and before the race was over a large part of the 9766 customers had started to leave. The spectators, enthusiastic about the regular stock car races, seemed bored by the late model cars."

Fans who didn't leave early witnessed a historic moment in Toronto. Placing 17th after starting seventh was another Petty, Lee's son Richard. While the "King" had raced in NASCAR's Convertible division earlier in the year, racing historians claim the Toronto race was the first major NASCAR event for the 21-year-old rookie.

Since 1958, Canada has been waiting for its next race at the Cup level. While NASCAR established a Canadian base of operations in

a partnership with television sports network TSN in 2004, no plans are underway to present a Cup race in Canada. There are no tracks suitable for an event, and the present 38-race schedule is very tight for adding races. "There is just not room for any added races," according to NASCAR Nextel Cup star Jimmie Johnson. "Right now we just get three weekends off a season."

NASCAR Canada also entered into a multi-year operational and marketing agreement with Canadian-based stock car series CASCAR (Canadian Association for Stock Car Auto Racing) late in 2004 to promote stock car racing at the grassroots level.

Close to 30 Canadians have competed in NASCAR's top level since Montrealer Albert Lemieux raced at Stamford Park in 1952. And for over 50 years, drivers such as Trevor Boys of Calgary, Roy Smith of Victoria, British Columbia, and Vic Parsons of Toronto have gone south to compete in the top level of stock car competition.

But of all these drivers, three Canadians stand above the rest. From the small Ontario town of Ailsa Craig, Earl Ross was a fixture on the short ovals. Between 1973 and 1976 Ross started in 26 Cup events, and he holds the distinction of being the only Canadian to win a race in NASCAR Cup competition. Driving for Junior Johnson, Ross won the Old Dominion 500 at Martinsville in 1974 in his Chevy.

Another Ontario driver tried his hand at the big show from 1966 to 1969. Based in Port Credit, Don Biederman entered 42 Cup races, with his best showing a seventh in the 1967 Nashville 400 in a Ron Stotten Chevy.

While his career in NASCAR Cup racing has been limited, Ron Fellows of Toronto has been a dominant driver on NASCAR road circuits, driving for teams such as Nemechek and DEI. Almost all of Fellows' dozen Cup races to date, since he first ran at Watkins Glen in 1995, have been on road courses. He has two second-place finishes, both at the Glen, in 1999 and 2004. In 2005 he drove in two events, with an eighth-place finish at Infineon. Fellows is also racing on the road circuits in 2006.

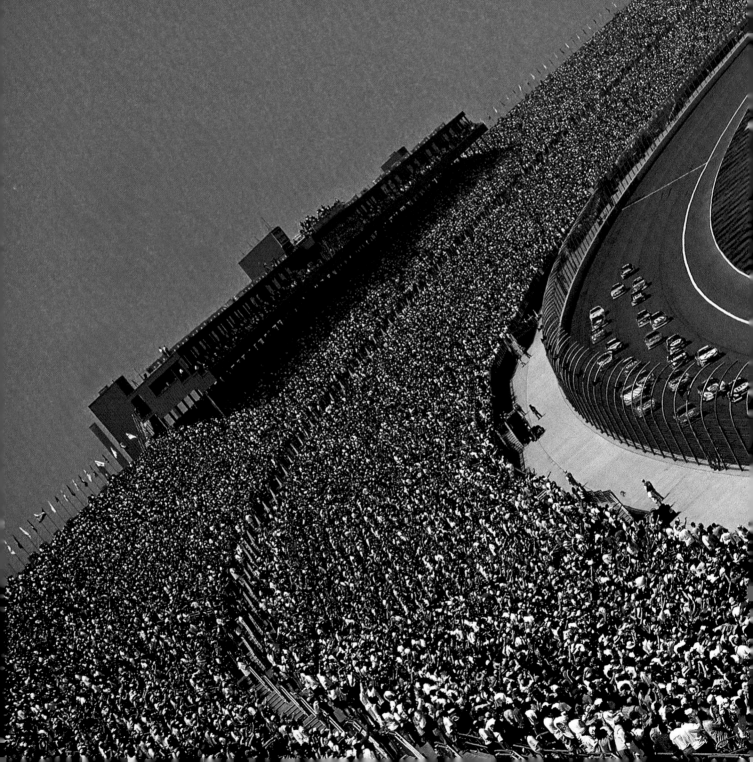

NASCAR 101

STOCK CARS

This shot exemplifies the speed, color and dynamics of stock car racing. Here Kasey Kahne leads during the Coca-Cola 600 at the Lowe's Motor Speedway in May 2006.

In the early years, a racer could literally go to an auto dealership, buy a car off the lot and go stock car racing. The earliest NASCAR stocks were usually the lightest, most powerful cars in a manufacturer's line of two-door sedans. Popular entries around 1950 were the Oldsmobile 88, with its recently introduced overhead valve engine, or Chrysler with its state-of-the-art Hemi-head engine from 1951.

These cars were heavy, and while a car's engine would last, other parts such as the suspension, brakes and drive train failed much of the time. One of the biggest trouble spots was in the tires. Not only were they skinny compared to today's tires, they were stock road tires, not built to withstand the excessive heat build-up, so blow-outs were very common.

In 1948, Hudson introduced its "Step-down" model, a bulbous vehicle with a wide stance and frame rails outside the rear wheels. Not only did this car sit lower than others, it offered superior handling characteristics for its day, and was very rugged.

Hudson did not have a V8 engine, but the carmaker did have an engineering department that saw the promotional value of stock car racing. When pioneer driver Marshall Teague came knocking at Hudson's Detroit plant, engineers worked with Teague to build a strong, dependable car. With its optional Hornet X7 engine, and special "export only" suspension

and brake package, the Hudson was a hard car to beat on the track in the early 1950s.

Other car manufacturers weren't going to sit around and let this six-cylinder upstart take all the prizes. Soon all makes were producing "export" brakes and suspensions, and with their more powerful V8 engines, Hudson's day was over by 1954.

The powerful Chrysler 300s dominated the tracks in the mid-50s, but the Big Three automakers, especially Chevrolet, had developed light, high-revving V8 engines that left the bigger, heavier cars in the dust. By 1960, Oldsmobile and Pontiac, each with its own engine, ran successfully with the Fords, Dodges and Chevrolets.

While engine development flourished in NASCAR's first decade, the cars became less and less like the "stock" cars they were to represent. The cars were still full-framed, but strengthened. The biggest brakes, wheels and suspensions were installed along with huge radiators. Four-speed transmissions were the norm. Bumpers were retained, but all trim and lights were removed. The glitzy and space-age look of stock dashboards gave way to a home-built panel. The interior was gutted, replaced with metal panels, one racing seat and roll-bar protection.

Driver safety was slow to evolve. All glass except for the windshield was removed, single roll bars were replaced with cages and padding was installed around the roll bars. There were no safety fuel cells in the early years. Eventually tire manufacturers developed racing-only tires – ones with wide profiles that could withstand punishment – but tire failure was still common.

As domestic cars changed from 1960 to about 1990, stock cars changed in regard to Detroit's yearly model turnover. NASCAR strictly controlled the horsepower race of the mid-1960s when engines such as Chrysler's 426-cubic-inch Hemi and Ford's overhead camshaft 427 appeared, and eventually prohibited their use. Wind-cheating body styles such as the Ford Torino and Dodge Charger became prominent, and were naturals for the superspeedway with their 200-plus mile-per-hour speeds. Full-size cars such as the Ford Galaxie and Chevrolet Impala were replaced by mid-sized cars with a shorter wheel base, such as the Chevrolet Monte Carlo, Buick Regal and Ford Thunderbird.

By 1990, Detroit did not offer a V8-powered, rear-wheel drive car suitable as a basis for NASCAR Cup racing. While some elements remain, the cars on today's speedways have little more than the name in common with today's street-driven, front-wheel drive, V6-powered sedans.

The work never stops. Tony Stewart's pit crew work on the Home Depot Chevrolet during practice at the UAW-GM Quality 500 at Lowe's Motor Speedway, October 2005.

TOYOTA CUP CAR

One of the world's automotive giants is going NASCAR Cup racing. Toyota announced early in 2006 that it will expand its NASCAR program by competing in the NASCAR Nextel Cup series, and the Busch Series, starting in 2007. This expansion follows three years of involvement in NASCAR's Craftsman Truck series. Toyota will base its Cup cars on its Camry model. It will join Dodge, Ford and Chevrolet in the stock car series.

Three teams will be fielded in this venture, and all are based in North Carolina. Bill Davis Racing has been a NASCAR competitor for 18 years in Cup and Busch racing, and the team has had three Tundra trucks in the Craftsman series since 2004.

Two-time Daytona 500 winner Michael Waltrip and his team will field Camrys in 2007. Waltrip formed his own team nine years ago, running in the Busch series. He plans to drive a NAPA-sponsored Camry.

And the third team is new to Cup racing. Team Red Bull will be headed by stock car veteran Marty Gaunt. Red Bull is not new to auto racing, as it presently owns and operates two Formula One teams.

Toyota has been involved in auto racing in North America for more than two decades in IMSA, CART, IRL and off-road competition. This will be the first time the auto maker will be racing with a car that has a general appearance to its street version, apart from a brief stint with a Celica in the Goody Dash Series in 2000.

Most racing ventures by Toyota have been in racing that highlights technical innovations. Although this may appear a move backwards in this area for Toyota, which must now design and build a race car based on a rear-wheel drive platform with a carburetor plunked down on the engine, Toyota's entry into NASCAR's top echelons is a smart move in terms of to marketing and brand awareness.

Although Japanese in origin, Toyota is committed as a North American-based auto maker, with several plants in North America building millions of vehicles, including more than 6.5 million Camrys from its Kentucky plant.

Today's NASCAR Car

The NASCAR Nextel Cup car of today blends the reliability and power of a V8 engine with a solid full frame and the most aerodynamic body the rules will allow. This package has been developed not only for winning, but to offer the utmost in safety.

Engines

Power plants are custom-made with very few factory parts by several racing engine manufacturers. Each piece of each engine is built with maximum endurance and power in mind. The engine block uses special alloys to provide more strength in key areas such as the main bearings. Cylinder heads are aluminum for light weight and valve-porting versatility, which allows the engine to breathe better, thus providing more power.

At present there are three engines in the top levels of stock car racing – from Ford, Chevrolet and Dodge. The displacement of these engines is 358 cubic inches, and they produce 750–800 horsepower, running high-octane gasoline through a huge carburetor. No fuel injection is allowed, and compression ratios are 12:1, much higher than a street car with ratios of anywhere from 8:1 to 9.5:1.

All these specialized engine parts allow a Nextel Cup car engine to withstand at least 8,000 rpm for hours at a time. Engines cost upwards of $40,000 each, and are hand-assembled, then run on a dynamometer, a calibration machine that informs mechanics and engineers of every aspect of an engine's behavior.

The most significant – and one of the most controversial – changes to NASCAR engines has been the use of a restrictor plate to slow down the cars. This plate is sandwiched between the carburetor and intake manifold, controlling the fuel/air flow mixture into the engine.

The four barrels of a Cup carburetor measure 1 9/16" in diameter. The restrictor plate has four holes of 29/32" in diameter, blocking some of the carburetor's larger holes; hence, the engine does not take in as much fuel, reducing the horsepower.

NASCAR CUP CAR SPECIFICATIONS

Eligible Models	Monte Carlo Dodge Charger Ford Taurus	Rear Suspension	Trailing arms, coil springs, Panhard bar
Years	2004–2006	Chassis	Rectangular steel tubing with integral roll cage
Engine	Cast-iron V-8, 358 cubic inch maximum displacement, with aluminum cylinder heads	Body Length	200.7 inches
		Body Width	72.5 inches
		Car height	51 inches (minimum)
Horsepower	850 at 9000 rpm (may vary at restrictor plate events)	Car weight	3400 pounds without driver
Compression Ratio	12:1	Front air dam	3.5 inches (may vary at restrictor plate events)
Torque	550 ft/lb at 7500 rpm	Gear ratios	2.90 to 6.50
Induction	One four-barrel carburetor (Holley)	Spoiler	55 inches wide by 4.5 inches high (may vary at restrictor plate races)
Top Speed	200 mph		
Transmission	Four-speed manual	Wheelbase	110 inches
Fuel	122-octane rating	Wheels	15 inches by 9.5 inches, steel
Front Suspension	Independent coil springs with upper and lower A-frames	Tread width	60.5 inches (maximum)
		Brakes	Disc, front and rear

Carl Edwards having a peek under the hood of his Ford between test sessions at Lowe's, May 2006.

Restrictor plates became mandatory at the Talladega and Daytona superspeedways in 1988 in an attempt to slow the cars down after some high-speed accidents. Some believe if restrictor plates were not used, Cup cars could achieve speeds of at least 225 mph on the larger tracks thanks to improved aerodynamics of the cars over the past decade.

Officials contend that restrictor plates help avoid high-speed crashes, but drivers complain that the plates cause multi-car pile-ups, as all cars are now so evenly matched that they race around the track in a tight group at 190 mph. If one car in a group loses control, or blows a tire or engine, it usually causes a chain reaction and takes out other racers.

Body – Chassis

Car bodies are based on American-made full-size passenger sedans, and have to look something like the models driven on the street. A body designation may be no more than three years old.

A car's frame consists of round and square tubing with the roll cage making up an integral part. The frame is designed in three sections: the front clip, the driver's compartment and the rear clip. The front and rear clip are collapsible and are intended to crush upon impact. The front clip is designed to push the engine down and out of the bottom of the car rather than back into the driver's area.

The body-building process is determined by NASCAR rules and must meet 30 designated contours as set out in official guidelines. Tolerances are tight, allowing for differentials between the official templates and the car body of 0.5 inches to 0.07 inches.

Several manufacturers' production panels, such as the roof and windshield posts, along with hoods, trunk lids and floor pans are used to build a race car body. Other areas such as the nose, tail, and rocker panel sections are plastic and come from after-market firms.

The fenders, doors and quarter panels are hand-formed in the race car shop and worked on until they match the regulation templates. Only sheet metal is allowed – no aluminum or fiberglass can be used.

When the body has been fitted to the chassis, all body parts are then welded together and smoothed out into one seamless piece. This allows for better aerodynamic flow. The body is then primed, painted and lettered.

A stock car's windshield is made of a poly-carbonate material called Lexan, which is very strong and used in aircraft applications. It is also a soft material, so it does not shatter. If an object is thrown up into the windshield, it will just scratch or dent the windshield, or imbed itself.

Race cars have had spoilers on their bodies for decades. This panel, along with a front-end air dam, is used to create downforce to help keep the car's stance on the track and improve traction.

In 1994 NASCAR introduced roof flaps, a safety device designed to keep a car from becoming airborne. Previously, at high speeds, a car would fly into the air if it rotated during its spin, resulting in some horrendous crashes. Roof flaps disrupt the air flow, keeping the car close to the ground.

Through wind-tunnel testing, these two flaps are recessed into the rear area of the roof. When a car reaches an angle of significant lift, the low pressure above the flaps sucks them open. The first flap is designed to open at a 140-degree angle from a car's centerline, and the second flap at a 180-degree angle, to make sure the air flow is curtailed as the car rotates.

Fuel Tanks

Bursting fuel tanks and fires were common in NASCAR's early years, resulting in driver fatalities and serious injury. Today's 22-gallon tanks, known as fuel cells, have built-in features to minimize ruptures and explosions.

A fuel cell is a product of aerospace technology. It consists of a metal box centered in the car's rear and anchored with four strong braces. Inside the steel outer layer is a flexible, tear-resistant bladder and foam baffling.

The foam reduces fuel sloshing around in the tank. It also reduces the amount of air in the cell, which lessens the chance of explosion. If the cell does ignite internally, the foam absorbs the explosion. The car also has check valves that shut off the fuel supply if the engine is separated from the car.

Kevin Lepage has some problems during the Crown Royal 400 in May 2006 at Richmond. This engine oil fire is dramatic, but doesn't help win races.

air, because nitrogen contains less moisture than compressed air. As heat builds up inside a tire, internal moisture evaporates and expands, causing the tire pressure to increase. Even a small amount of pressure difference will affect a car's handling capabilities. By using nitrogen, race teams have more control over pressure buildup.

On race tracks longer than one mile, NASCAR rules require tires to contain an inner liner as a safety precaution. This inner tire is essentially a second tire mounted on the wheel inside the regular tire, and it allows the driver better control on the still-intact inner tire if the outer tire blows during a race.

The material used in making the tire – its compound – is different for each race track. Softer compounds provide a better grip but wear out more quickly than a harder compound. NASCAR and tire company engineers have studied compounds and determined the most suitable for each racing venue, according to track surface and abrasiveness, number of turns, and the banking degrees of those turns.

A tire used on a road course, where the car must turn both left and right, will be different from a tire used on an oval short track with only tight left-hand corners.

The Driver's Compartment

Everything inside the driver's compartment has a purpose. There are no frills or luxuries in this cocoon of roll bars, padding and painted sheet metal.

First and foremost, a stock car's interior is built for safety. The roll cage is made of heavy tubing and is an integral part of the car. It can withstand severe punishment, and is a testament to the dedication of safety rules in racing. A car may be involved in a severe mishap such as hitting a retaining wall, getting jostled around with other cars, or flipping over several times, but the driver is insulated within this strong cage, and usually walks away.

There are other items inside the car which help keep the driver safe within the roll cage. The driver's seat is designed and manufactured

Tire wear and management is considered a science or a black art in NASCAR. But data acquisition on tires has become an important part of a car's success.

Tires

Of all the components on a race car, the tires are probably the most different from those on a passenger car. Race car tires are black, and of a radial design, but that's about it for similarities.

A race car tire is about 12 inches wide, and treadless. Both of these characteristics provide more traction and grip on the paved racing surface. The tires are built exclusively for racing, cost about $350 each, and last on average 75 to 100 miles. They are sticky to the touch, giving them a better grip, and weigh less than street car tires.

Race car tires are filled with nitrogen, not

to keep the driver from hitting anything during a crash. The seat is almost an extension of the driver, and is molded to fit the body like a glove. The seat will also absorb some of a crash's energy by bending upon impact.

Seats are formed to wrap around a driver's ribcage, and some newer seats wrap around the driver's shoulders as well. When the seat is wrapped tightly around the ribcage, it provides greater support in a crash, spreading the load over the entire ribcage rather than concentrating on a small area. As well as rib and shoulder supports, seats have head supports on their right side, giving the driver's head and neck a solid brace for going around left-handed corners hours at a time.

The seat belt system is much more complex and robust than the unit in the average street car. The five-point harness restraint is designed to hold the driver tightly in his seat so his movement is restricted to the motion of the car. Made of thick padded webbing, the harness attaches at a central point in the driver's lap. Two straps come down over the driver's shoulders, two straps come around his waist, and one comes up between the legs.

As race cars became more sophisticated over the years, window glass was taken from the car for weight and safety purposes. This allowed great air flow into the interior, but if the car was involved in a crash, especially a roll-over, the driver's arms could flail out the door opening and be crushed. Window nets, a nylon mesh webbing, were mandated, and this safety device covers the driver's door window opening to keep the racer's arms inside the car in the event of an accident.

A race car has no doors, so a driver climbs into the cockpit through the driver's window area. As the driver sits in his seat, the steering wheel is fastened to the collapsible steering column. The wheel is removable for ease of entry and exit.

Inside the car, there is no padded dashboard with chrome trim and name plates. Instead, on a flat homemade panel there are several toggle switches and instruments. No keys are needed. With a flip of the ignition switch and a press on the starter button, the engine roars to life. There is a switch to turn on a fan to cool the rear brakes when necessary, a switch to turn on the radiator fan when needed, and a blower

Kurt Busch all tucked in and ready to roll. Today's drivers have come a long way in the safety department since the days of t-shirts, loafers and sunglasses.

A driver can tell in an instant what is happening with this bevy of instruments. Those toggle switches wouldn't pass any highway safety standards though.

fan switch to bring outside air into the driver's area.

Race cars have no speedometers. The oil pressure gauge will show 70–80 psi (pounds per square inch) if the engine is running well at speed, and the oil temperature gauge will register 250°F to 270°F. Under good conditions, the water temperature gauge will read 190°F to 210°F, and, like a street car, if the gauge reads over 220°F there's a problem in the cooling system.

A stock car does not have a fuel level gauge, but it has a fuel pressure gage, which is a diagnostic-type unit that shows any irregularities in fuel delivery from the fuel cell to the engine. The ideal pressure is seven or eight psi.

Other gauges include a voltmeter, which displays the car's electrical charging system, and works like a street car voltmeter. If the needle is reading only nine volts with a 12-volt battery system, then the alternator or other electrical device is faulty, and the battery will eventually go flat. Completing the gauge package is the tachometer, an instrument that displays the engine speed in revolutions per minute.

When at speed on a track, drivers use their experience and instinct about engine speed to shift gears. But with no speedometer, and speed limits imposed on entering and leaving pit road, the driver will note his RPMs to keep his speed within these limits.

Competition Updates

NASCAR is continually updating competition elements in its Nextel Cup racing. Here are some of the highlights that have taken place since 2004.

➤ **Rear spoilers** on Cup cars have been reduced by an inch at all non-restrictor plate races, and this measurement was set at 4.5 inches in 2005. This change was made to further reduce the aero-push and provide better passing ability. Car spoilers for restrictor plate tracks such as Daytona and Talladega are 6.75 inches high.

➤ **Restrictor plates** at Daytona and Talladega were reduced in 2005 by $\frac{1}{64}$ of an inch to $\frac{57}{64}$ of an inch from the $\frac{29}{32}$ of an inch used in 2004.

Looking bare and forlorn without the sponsor logos, a group of cars test at Daytona in 2006 in the only restrictor-plate test session allowed.

↝ **The provisional system** for race qualifying changed. Teams no longer accrue provisional throughout the season to gain entry into starting fields. Positions one through 42 are still determined by qualifying speed, but these will be the 35 highest-ranked positions on Cup series owner points prior to the entry deadline, providing the team has made an attempt to qualify. The remaining seven positions of the grid are assigned to the drivers with the fastest qualifying speeds whose car owners are not in the top-35 ranking. The final or 43rd starting spot goes to the car owner whose driver is a current or past NASCAR Cup champion. For the first five races of the season, the previous season's points will determine this provisional procedure, and from the sixth race on, the current owner points will determine the top-35 ranking.

↝ **With an eye to keeping engine speeds down,** NASCAR officials changed rear axle gear ratios that limit engine revolutions and provide more reliability in engines. NASCAR will determine these ratios at each track except Daytona and Talladega, where restrictor plates are in use to limit car speed. In an associated move, NASCAR equips each car with a data-logging device that measures engine speeds during all on-track activity.

That's crew chief Slugger Labbe setting up the rear spoiler on an Evernham Dodge before the 2005 Allstate 400 at the Brickyard.

↝ **NASCAR will impound race cars** that have qualified for an event until race day, and in most cases, teams will not be allowed to work on their cars. This new procedure altered the traditional weekend schedule, including the elimination of the two 45-minute practices after qualifying, commonly known as "Happy Hour."

SAFETY

He may think they're wasting time, but Kurt Busch is waiting while officials check his Dodge after an on-track incident. Safety is paramount in NASCAR.

The basic premise of an auto race is simple. Win the race. But also uppermost in racing today is safety. Drivers and cars are subjected to punishment that not only destroys cars but could lead to serious driver injury and death if not for the safety equipment in place on the car, on the driver himself, and on the race track.

Aside from the vault-like safety of a race car's roll cage, driving suit and restraint system, the driver is protected in other ways.

Driver Equipment

Stock car drivers are sheltered from head to toe before taking to the track. They wear several pieces of protective gear that could prove lifesaving in case of an accident.

The head is the most vulnerable part of the body. As in other sports, the competitor's helmet is designed to dissipate impact energy and prevent outside elements from puncturing it. Attached to the front of the helmet is a full face shield, protecting the eyes.

A racing helmet has three parts: the outer shell, the outer liner and the inner liner. The outer shell is made from gel coat, special resins, carbon, and substances such as Kevlar that form an extremely hard and durable surface. The outer liner is a special foam layer in the helmet's crown, made of polystyrene or polypropylene. This layer helps absorb shock energy not isolated by the outer shell.

Left: The "King" tries a NASA-inspired water-cooled helmet back in 1973. This helmet never caught on. Richard Petty didn't need it anyway – he was the coolest driver on the tracks.

Right: Head attire is not only safe, it's colorful and unique. And it's a lot safer than the strap-on, loose-fitting helmets of the early years.

Bottom: A major safety breakthrough has been the HANS (Head and Neck Support) device for drivers of all types of racing.

The inner liner is a form-fitting layer of a fire-retardant material of nylon, or Nomex, made by DuPont Chemical. This material does not burn, melt or support combustion.

Cheek pads and chin straps on the helmet are also fireproof. The face shield is made of the tough but pliable Lexan plastic that is also used for the windshields of a Cup car.

The threat of a car fire has diminished over the years, but is still possible. Fire-retardant material such as Proban or Nomex is woven into the materials used to make the driving suit, gloves, socks and shoes worn by the driver. The suits are rated in protecting drivers from second-degree gasoline fire burns, with time ranges between three and 40 seconds.

The latest innovation in personal driver safety is the HANS (Head and Neck Support) device. This apparatus was designed to reduce the chance of injury caused by unrestrained movement of a driver's head during a crash. Built of carbon fiber and Kevlar, the HANS device is a semi-hard collar weighing 1.5 pounds, which is held onto the upper body by a harness worn by the driver. Two flexible tethers attach the collar to the helmet to

prevent the head from snapping forward or sideways.

Developed by engineering professor Dr. Robert Hubbard and sports car racer Jim Downing, the HANS device was initially accepted and proven in other forms of motorsport, but not stock car racing. But the deaths of NASCAR Cup drivers Adam Petty, Kenny Irwin, Tony Roper and Dale Earnhardt since May 2000 have changed this view. All four were killed when their cars slammed into a wall and the drivers suffered fractures to the base of the skull. In October 2001 NASCAR mandated a head and neck restraint for drivers in all its classes.

Retaining Walls

While there are Nextel Cup races at many different tracks, all tracks have one thing in common – concrete retaining walls. These walls contain cars within the racing area in the event of a crash or loss of control. The walls,

however, do not absorb any energy or have any give, making any contact with them possibly treacherous. To rectify this potentially dangerous situation, energy-absorbing barriers of crushable material have been installed at some tracks to dissipate the force of the impact. At present there are several types of these "soft walls" at race tracks.

A block of foam surrounded by polystyrene, known as Cello foam, has been used at the Lowe's Motor Speedway in turns two and four with good results. Another soft wall system, championed by the Indy Racing League (IRL) and used at the Indianapolis Motors Speedway, is PEDS (polyethylene energy dissipation system). This involves small polyethylene cylinders installed inside larger ones, absorbing the impact of a crashing car.

The Impact Protection System (IPS) is a soft wall design made of layered PVC material with an integrated honeycomb structure. The inner piece of this wall is then wrapped in a rubber casing. These walls are segmented and attached to the concrete walls with cables.

The newest proposal in this development at stock car speedways is the SAFER (Steel and Foam Energy Reduction) system. Developed by the University of Nebraska, this system comprises four steel tubes welded into 20-foot sections. It is then bolted to the wall with hard pink foam between itself and the outer concrete wall.

Of the 20 oval tracks in NASCAR Cup competition, almost all now have the SAFER system in place. It has been installed on a 3,000-foot section in turn four of Talledaga Speedway, and the track plans to have the entire racing perimeter set up with the SAFER system. Dover finished its installation in 2005, and at present Bristol has yet to implement the barrier. The two road courses on the Cup schedule, Watkins Glen and Infineon, present unique challenges in using the system, and the use of the SAFER wall system at these circuits is under evaluation.

The soft wall technology has not been fully accepted. Some flaws in the systems have been cited. If a wall of a breakable material is hit, then there is a time delay in cleaning up the pieces and replacing the damaged area.

Another criticism is that a car can bounce off a soft wall back into oncoming traffic – with disastrous results. Also, with Cup cars driving so close to the wall to get the best racing line when setting up for the turns, a car could scrape against the soft wall at such an angle that it could get caught in the material and lose control.

As a testament to the strong, heavily protected driver's compartment in today's NASCAR vehicle, Ryan Newman walked away after the car got airborne and rolled three times before stopping on its roof. Note the rear axle is missing from the Alltel Dodge. "I was just in the wrong place at the wrong time," said Newman after the 2003 Daytona 500 accident. "I'll tell you this, Disney World doesn't have anything like that."

Opposite: Along with foam walls, "givable" restraints such as this fence keep drivers and cars in much better shape than concrete walls when a mishap occurs.

PIT STOPS

Colorful, vibrant and packed with action, pit stops have become a fan favorite and in some instances can be more exciting than the race itself.

Pit stops are an important and integral part of a race. What was once a leisurely activity for refueling and getting new tires has turned into a series of highly disciplined skills, where time and teamwork are of the essence. An event can be won or lost in a pit stop.

When a race car comes into the pits for service, what appears to be semi-organized chaos is actually a well-rehearsed routine like no other. Moving in compete harmony, seven team members jump over the pit wall with their tools and equipment to fuel the car, change tires and perform other on-the-spot duties such as suspension adjustments.

All this is performed in under 18 seconds, and then the race car is back on its way. Try to get 22 gallons of gas, four new tires and the windshield cleaned in that time at your local service station.

Jack Man

This team member is the first and last person to touch the car when in the pits. The jack man is ready with a lightweight (35-pound) aluminum jack and has the car's right side up in the air almost before the car comes to a complete stop. A good jack man gets the car up with one-and-a-half pumps on the jack lever. He then stays with the car to make sure it remains stable during the tire changes, and keeps the loose tires out of the way. He also helps the rear tire changer in discarding the used tires.

Driver changes are very rare in NASCAR, but an ailing Tony Stewart is helped out of his Chevy at Dover in June 2006. Ricky Rudd took over the driving.

When the right side is complete, he rushes to the driver's side and performs the same duties; and when all team members have completed their tasks, he lets the car down, which is the signal to the driver to exit the pits.

Gas Man

The gas man is one of a two-person team, and his duty is to manually fill the race car's fuel cell with up to 22 gallons of fuel. Using two 11-gallon containers, the gas man rams the container's spring-loaded neck into the car's fuel cell plate, which is also spring-loaded. When these connect, a vacuum is created that allows for maximum fuel flow from the container into the fuel cell. This way there is no backflow – something that could happen when you're filling your average car at a service station, causing gas to spill all over your clothes and shoes.

Catch Can Man

This team member assists the gas man by holding the first 11-gallon container in place on the car while the gas man readies the second container. He also operates a flap on a one-inch pipe that leads to the fuel cell in the car. By opening this flap, air is forced out of the fuel cell so the maximum amount of fuel can be loaded. If there is any overflow, the excess fuel will be pushed out of this small pipe and caught in a can. For obvious reasons, both the gas man and the catch can man wear fire-retardant clothing.

Tire Changers

There are two tire changers on each team. One changes the front tires, and the other changes the rear tires. When a car is in the air, the changer quickly removes the tire using an air gun. The new tires and wheels have their five lug nuts stuck on the wheel beforehand to speed up fastening them to the car. Although the changers' tools are called air guns, they operate on nitrogen rather than compressed air. Nitrogen is used because compressed air contains moisture that could damage these guns.

Tire Carriers

These two crew members carry the 60-pound front and rear tires and wheels to the race car, and also assist the tire changers. A carrier will help a changer in case there's a stuck wheel, and the front tire carrier will clean away any debris from the front of the car while the jackman is changing sides. The carriers always ensure that a discarded tire is laid flat on the pavement so it doesn't roll away into a moving race car or another team member.

Try to get 22 gallons of gas, four new tires and the windshield cleaned in 18 seconds at your service station.

Crew member Murray Timm in full battle dress.

Inside a Pit Stop

As with most features in the sport of NASCAR Nextel Cup racing, car preparation has evolved from a casual, backyard type of atmosphere into a highly organized, costly and professional enterprise that is continuously being updated in a team's pursuit to win races.

And one of the biggest changes in Cup racing has been the development of pit stops. What was once a one-time semi-planned, off-the-cuff approach to changing tires and adding fuel during a race is now an important factor in a team's achievement, and successful pit stops can win races for a team.

The process of changing tires, throwing in a couple of cans of fuel and wiping the wind-shield, which used to take minutes, can now be accomplished in 15 seconds. But this has not evolved overnight. Pit stops take skill, dedica-tion, teamwork and practice. Lots of practice.

As front tire changer for the Kyle Busch-driven, Kellogg's-sponsored Chevy of Hendrick Motorsports, Murray Timm is one of these dedicated team members. Along with the rest of the "over the wall" crew, Timm performs his duties to the utmost for 36 Sundays a year during the NASCAR Nextel Cup season.

But if you think this is easy, glorified

employment with lots of travel, think again. Performing on a pit crew at this level is almost non-stop work, according to Timm, who has been with HMS for 10 years. "Not only do we work out three, four times a week, we are always practicing," said Timm, who also "hangs bodies" (works as a car body fabrica-tor) at the 70-acre racing facility in Charlotte, North Carolina.

"We practice, practice, practice," added Timm. "For a while I went to bed, closed my eyes and went to sleep with visions of an air gun in my hand hitting lug nuts. Now I have my skills in line," he went on. "I can do it with my eyes shut. But I still practice."

As well as fabricating car bodies during the week, Timm and the rest of his team have three or four pit stop practice sessions a week. "Four sessions is enough," he added. "After five we're worn out and we're starting to fade."

To help the team maintain its physical and mental edge, a personal trainer works with the squad during the week, similar to other major league sports. While the trainer does not attend the races, the crew can often be seen doing sit-ups and other calisthenics before and during a race.

And for each race weekend, the team has a coach on site who keeps it focused and positive. Not only does the coach mentor the team during the weekend, he times pit practice sessions and helps members with their exercising.

The trainer Timm and his crew work with is an ex-NFL coach. Timm said some Cup teams have tried athletes such as football play-ers to perform pit crew duties, but added this was not a viable option as Cup teams need mechanically inclined individuals rather than athletes.

As part of the Number 5 car's "late crew," Timm and his team fly out of the Concord, North Carolina, airport around 3:30 a.m. of race day if the event is east of Texas. For a western race such as Fontana or Phoenix, the crew flies out Saturday night.

At the track at 7 a.m. of race day, Timm and his group take over from the other eight

members who got to the track the previous Wednesday with the cars and parts and equipment for the initial setup.

So Sunday morning, Timm helps unload the gear needed for the race at pitside in the team's assigned spot on pit road. Then it's off to the Goodyear Tire compound area, returning with 12 to 14 sets of tires for the race. These tires must then be cleaned up and prepped.

By 10:30, all preparations are complete, and the team gets ready for the big show, donning their uniforms, checking radios, and working on a multitude of last-minute details and strategies in readiness for the green flag.

Even with 10 years' experience, Timm said he still experiences pre-race jitters. But once the green flag drops, it's down to business. All crew members are in constant contact with each other during a race. Timm added that in a typical race there are eight stops on average. Some tracks, such as Darlington, require up to 12 stops.

No matter what the race, the crew works on its skills between pit stops, staying as alert and prepared as possible. And the hours of practice pay off when the driver brings his car in for servicing, as seven athletes jump the wall, change all four tires, and get 22 gallons of fuel in the car in about 15 of the most orchestrated seconds in any sport.

Timm mentioned that a pit crew's mental approach is not only dependent on how the team is faring during the actual race, but on how the team's driver is performing and his frame of mind during the contest.

"The driver's attitude plays with you," he said. "And if you have missed the set-up you try harder to help the driver because you know he's not able to perform to the best of his ability."

Timm said the training and practice really pay off during the night races on the Cup circuit. "During the night races it's hard to see. Sometimes the brake dust is so thick you just can't see the lug nuts when changing the tire and wheel. This is where the mechanical skills and practice come in."

As a team member, the race can be exhilarating or frustrating, said Timm, especially when the team's outcome can be decided on so many outside factors, such as mechanical problems.

"It's hard on us not to finish," he admitted. "But the winning is overwhelming. It was pretty cool when Kyle won both California and Phoenix in 2005."

Timm believes the camaraderie with his co-workers at Hendrick produces solid results to the team's efforts. "Attitudes and chemistry are important," he stated. "We're all friends. We spend more time together than we do with our family."

That's Timm working on the left front wheel. A 10-year over-the-wall veteran, his skills are honed. "I can do it with my eyes shut. But I still practice."

THE BUSINESS OF NASCAR

The crowd at Bristol: A packed house.

In 1949, the first full year of NASCAR racing, Robert "Red" Byron won the championship title and about $5,800. Byron raced until 1952, had 15 starts and won a lifetime total of $10,100.

In 2005 NASCAR Nextel Cup champ Tony Stewart won over $13.5 million.

This is a vivid demonstration of how NASCAR has grown from its humble rural roots into a series of lucrative two- and three-day events in most of the larger U.S. urban centers.

To appreciate the financial juggernaut the NASCAR Nextel Cup series has become, Stewart's winnings are a single-season record payout in the history of the sport. The Indiana driver won just over $6 million in point fund awards alone, on top of his race winnings of $6.9 million, plus another $517,000 in special awards.

Stewart's winnings exceed the previous single-season record of almost $11 million, won by Jeff Gordon in 2001.

Gordon, who placed 11th in the 2005 standings, won a season total of $7.9 million and is NASCAR's top money earner, with $74,887,079 at the close of the 2005 season.

Three veterans are next on the list. Mark Martin has amassed close to $54 million, Dale Jarrett is next with just over $52 million, and Rusty Wallace has taken home $49.7 million.

With his successful 2005 season, Stewart

is now fifth in all-time earnings with $48.4 million. In regular race earnings for 2005 alone, 40 of the 88 drivers/teams listed in NASCAR Cup competition earned over $1 million each. Terry Labonte finished in 40th spot and won $1.2 million.

Where does this money come from?

Tickets

Over seven million fans have been buying tickets to one or more of the 36 annual NASCAR Cup races for several years now. With 23 tracks on the circuit, Darlington holds 65,000 fans, while at the other end, Indianapolis Motor Speedway seats 250,000 fans. Of these 23 venues, 11 facilities hold more than 100,000 people.

In 1959 a spectator ticket in the Oldfield section at Daytona was $8. Now the same seat costs about $150. If you want a premium viewing of the 500, expect to pay a premium price of close to $1,000 at the start–finish line in the Nextel Tower.

Television

Aside from fans paying at the turnstiles for the 36 races, huge sponsorships, contingency awards and product marketing rights, a lot of NASCAR's funding is provided by television coverage.

Late in 2005 the stock car series completed an eight-year deal with several broadcast media, including Fox, Turner, ABC and ESPN, starting in 2007. As examples, ABC/ESPN will air 17 races a year, costing the network $270 million, and Fox will pay $208 million for 13 events a year.

Of the $4.4 billion television deal, about 65 percent of the money will go to the race tracks themselves. The Cup teams will receive about 25 percent, and NASCAR will get about 10 percent.

A television commercial during the 1979 Daytona 500 broadcast cost between $25,000 and $30,000. The same air time now costs advertisers upwards of $200,000.

Carl Edwards in practice at Lowe's, May 2006, with a sky behind him nearly blotted out with billboards.

Right: One of NASCAR's most expensive billboards. The "TV panel," shown here on Jimmie Johnson's Chevy, can fetch up to $1 million per season.

Below: Jimmie Johnson with his fans. NASCAR fans are some of the most devoted in any sport.

Sponsorship

Corporations spend an estimated $1 billion annually in sponsorships and promotions in NASCAR Cup racing. Title sponsor Nextel Communications signed a 10-year agreement with NASCAR in 2004 worth $750 million.

And this money is welcomed by the race teams, who spend an estimated $1 million per team each season for tires alone. The average cost for a ready-to-race engine is about $60,000, and the rest of the car can cost up to $70,000.

In the early 1960s the average per-race sponsorship cost was about $200. Now it's close to $400,000, so you can see why a primary sponsorship with a race team can cost between $3 and $6 million per season.

Cars have become very fast and very expensive rolling billboards. For a primary sponsorship, the corporation gets its product name on the car's hood and quarter panels. A company logo on the car's trunk lid, known as the "TV panel" because it can be seen from the following car's television camera, can cost up to $1 million.

At the other end of the sponsorship scale, a 20-inch sticker situated on the car's sides costs a paltry $2,000 per race, but since it has to be there for each of the season's 36 races, this adds up to an annual cost of $72,000.

POINTS & SCORING

Starting in 2004, NASCAR officials modified the scoring system for the Nextel Cup. The previous system, which had been in place since 1975, was altered to add more excitement and to put an emphasis on winning races. Officials hope these modifications will generate more enthusiasm for the sport as the season progresses, as attendance and television ratings have traditionally dropped off in the fall.

In previous years, a team could claim the championship through consistency rather than winning more of the races. Matt Kenseth took the 2003 championship with only one victory, while Ryan Newman captured a series-high eight wins the same year but placed sixth.

In the new scoring system, after the first 26 races of the 36-race season, the teams in the top-10 in points standings – as well as any other teams within 400 points of the leader – will earn the right to take part in the "Chase for the Championship."

Drivers who qualify will have their points adjusted. The first-place team will begin the final 10 races with 5,050 points, the second team 5,045 points and so on, with incremental drops of five points for the remainder of the drivers.

Points

The points system in Nextel Cup competition may seem complicated at first, but it is a

Jimmie Johnson shows his appreciation after winning the Aaron's 499 at Talladega in May 2006.

After each race, points are distributed as follows:

PLACE	POINTS	PLACE	POINTS	PLACE	POINTS	PLACE	POINTS
1st	180	12th	127	23rd	94	34th	61
2nd	170	13th	124	24th	91	35th	58
3rd	165	14th	121	25th	88	36th	55
4th	160	15th	118	26th	85	37th	52
5th	155	16th	115	27th	82	38th	49
6th	150	17th	112	28th	79	39th	46
7th	146	18th	109	29th	76	40th	43
8th	142	19th	106	30th	73	41st	40
9th	138	20th	103	31st	70	42nd	37
10th	134	21st	100	32nd	67	43rd	34
11th	130	22nd	97	33rd	64		

thorough and fair system that also offers bonus points throughout the season.

Every one of the 36 Cup races is worth the same amount of points (except the special Bud Shootout and "The Winston," which do not qualify). There are no "unimportant" races on the schedule, so teams must perform their best at each race, whether it's the Daytona 500 or the Sharpie 500 at Bristol.

Bonus points are an important part of any race and can help a driver's standings:

- Any driver who leads any lap of a race gets five bonus points.
- The driver who leads the most laps of the race gets five bonus points.

OFFICIALS

Along with all the teams and thousands of fans at a Nextel Cup event, an important and necessary part of any race is the officiating staff.

A large team of dedicated men and women travel each week to every race to operate, score and officiate. There's more to running a race than just a person waving flags at the start/finish line. Dozens of officials register entrants, inspect the race cars to guarantee they meet rulebook standards, score each competitor during the race and ensure the track and its environs are absolutely first-rate for safe racing.

Here's a breakdown on some of the sanctioning body's duties.

Race Control

Located in a tower with a good view of the track, this is the heart and nerve center of a race. All decisions are made here regarding all aspects of the race operation. It is here that officials "call" the race, telling the flag person and corner workers when the race starts or when there's an incident on the track requiring a caution period.

An important part of race control is the scoring team. This group collects data on each race car once the race begins, and records each car's progress as the event progresses. Not only is this process recorded visually with video, but four methods are used to ensure the utmost in reliable, honest race information. NASCAR

The race starter on the podium, shown here at the 2004 Daytona 500, has the most important duties on race day. He is "the man" during an event.

Opposite: A powerful image of NASCAR: a track, a scoreboard and a green flag.

THE FLAG STAND

One of auto racing's most dominant visions is the flag waving. In NASCAR racing, an official starter is placed in a special stand directly above the track's start/finish line. Keeping constant radio contact with race control, the starter administers the running of the race through the use of a set of flags. Each flag has a specific purpose and is universal throughout all forms of motor sports.

 GREEN: Used at the beginning of a race, and at restarts. As with a green traffic light on city streets, this means the track is clear and racing may proceed.

 YELLOW: Denotes a caution period where the track is not clear as deemed by race officials. The yellow flag is displayed for an accident, track debris or unfavorable weather conditions. In most cases, cars must maintain their positions at the time this flag is displayed, and passing is not allowed. However, caution laps count as real laps.

 RED: Signifies there is a situation on the racetrack which is unsafe, and cars must stop as quickly as possible. This flag may appear when an incident occurs that mandates the use of safety or repair crews, if the track is blocked or, in stock car racing, a heavy rain makes track conditions unsafe to continue.

 BLUE WITH YELLOW: This is an information flag, and it is waved at a driver who is about to be overtaken by a faster car. Usually the driver of the slower car will make room to be overtaken at the first available opportunity.

 BLACK: The black flag is displayed to an individual car due to a mechanical problem noted by officials or a rules infraction. A car must enter the pits when black-flagged.

 WHITE: Signifies there is one lap remaining in a race.

 BLACK WITH WHITE: Shown to a car that refuses to pit after several laps of black-flag racing. If the driver does not acknowledge this condition, officials cease to score for the car in question.

 YELLOW WITH RED: Used on road courses, this flag is displayed by course workers at any given position on the course, signifying a track condition nearby that poses a potential hazard, such as oil on the track or a car blocking the course.

 CHECKERED: Waved at the end of the race when the scheduled distance has been completed.

uses transponders, electronic buttons, manual (visual) scoring and automatic scoring.

Transponders are small devices, about the size of a pack of playing cards, which are affixed to each car in the race. These devices constantly transmit signals to the scorers, and the signals are decoded by computers.

Another scoring method involves the electronic button system. Each competing team provides a person who activates this counting system by pushing a button every time his or her team's car crosses the track's scoring line in the race. This may be repetitious, but is a necessity and involves a great deal of concentration.

Then there's the old tried-and-true method of physically tallying each lap of a car by hand on a lap chart, a method used since the dawn of auto racing, and which still has its place even in today's computerized environment.

The final scoring method, which is used as a backup procedure only if necessary, is a computer-generated program that records the progress of each race car from flag to flag for the entire race.

Inspection

Technical inspection is an important aspect of stock car racing. Starting when the teams first roll into the track days before the actual race, inspectors armed with special tools and equipment check every piece of every car from engine specifications to tire sizes to body panel configuration. Through these inspections all cars race on an equal basis. Winning cars are also "torn down" (semi-dismantled) to ensure all parts are within regulations.

Pit Road

Pit stops play an exciting and important role in stock car racing, and officials are constantly working on pit row, monitoring the pit stops and enforcing the rules that govern proper pit stop procedures.

The pit road officials also monitor to the control tower and respective team crew chiefs, noting any potential problems while the car is in the pits for servicing.

TRACKS

The Nextel Cup comprises 36 races at 22 different tracks in the United States. Far from the small dirt tracks and beach races of the past, today's races are held at state-of-the-art facilities ranging in track size from just over half a mile, like Martinsville and Bristol, to the over two-mile superspeedways of Daytona and Talladega.

While the majority of the races are run on oval-configuration tracks, there are two road-racing circuits on the schedule which highlight the Cup cars and drivers in a nontraditional setting.

The season kicks off on February 15 with the Daytona 500 – considered to be the greatest race on the schedule – and runs almost every Sunday thereafter to the season-ending Ford 400 at the Homestead-Miami Speedway on November 21.

The majority of the tracks feature amenities such as private suites and boxes, upscale food concession stands and manufacturers' midways. Permanent fan seating ranges from 65,000 at Darlington Raceway to 250,000 seats at the Indianapolis Motor Speedway for the Brickyard 400. All Nextel Cup races are broadcast live on television and radio.

Richmond, May 2006. Tight, close racing – and tight, close seating.

ATLANTA MOTOR SPEEDWAY

Hampton, Ga.

TYPE: Oval

SIZE: 1.54 miles

BANKING IN CORNERS: 24°

DATE BUILT: 1959

FIRST CUP RACE: 1972

SEATING CAPACITY: 124,000

EVENTS: Golden Corral 500, Bass Pro Shops MBNA 500

BRISTOL MOTOR SPEEDWAY

Bristol, Tenn.

TYPE: Oval

SIZE: 0.533 miles

BANKING IN CORNERS: 36°

DATE BUILT: 1961

FIRST CUP RACE: 1972

SEATING CAPACITY: 160,000

EVENTS: Food City 500, Sharpie 500

CALIFORNIA SPEEDWAY

Fontana, Calif.

TYPE: D-shaped oval

SIZE: 2 miles

BANKING IN CORNERS: 14°

DATE BUILT: 1997

FIRST CUP RACE: 1997

SEATING CAPACITY: 92,000

EVENTS: Auto Club 500, Sony HD 500

CHICAGOLAND SPEEDWAY

Joliet, Ill.

TYPE: Tri-oval

SIZE: 1.5 miles

BANKING IN CORNERS: 18°

DATE BUILT: 2001

FIRST CUP RACE: 2001

SEATING CAPACITY: 75,000

EVENT: USG Sheetrock 400

DARLINGTON RACEWAY

Darlington, S.C.

TYPE: Oval

SIZE: 1.366 miles

BANKING IN CORNERS: 25°

DATE BUILT: 1949

FIRST CUP RACE: 1972

SEATING CAPACITY: 65,000

EVENT: Dodge Charger 500

DAYTONA INTERNATIONAL SPEEDWAY

Daytona Beach, Fla.

TYPE: Tri-oval

SIZE: 2.5 miles

BANKING IN CORNERS: 31°

DATE BUILT: 1959

FIRST CUP RACE: 1959

SEATING CAPACITY: 165,000

EVENTS: Budweiser Shootout, Gatorade Duel 1, Gatorade Duel 2, Daytona 500, Pepsi 400

DOVER INTERNATIONAL SPEEDWAY

Dover, Del.

TYPE: Oval

SIZE: 1.0 miles

BANKING IN CORNERS: 24°

DATE BUILT: 1969

FIRST CUP RACE: 1972

SEATING CAPACITY: 140,000

EVENT: Neighborhood Excellence 400 presented by Bank of America, Dover 400

HOMESTEAD-MIAMI SPEEDWAY

Homestead, Fla.

TYPE: Oval

SIZE: 1.5 miles

BANKING IN CORNERS: 20°

DATE BUILT: 1995

FIRST CUP RACE: 1999

SEATING CAPACITY: 72,000

EVENT: Ford 400

INDIANAPOLIS MOTOR SPEEDWAY

Speedway, Ind.

TYPE: Oval

SIZE: 2.5 miles

BANKING IN CORNERS: 9°

DATE BUILT: 1909

FIRST CUP RACE: 1994

SEATING CAPACITY: 250,000

EVENT: Allstate 400 at the Brickyard

INFINEON RACEWAY

Sonoma, Calif.

TYPE: Road course

SIZE: 1.99 miles

BANKING IN CORNERS: varies

DATE BUILT: 1968

FIRST CUP RACE: 1989

SEATING CAPACITY: varies

EVENT: Dodge/Save Mart 350

KANSAS SPEEDWAY

Kansas City, Kan.

TYPE: Tri-oval

SIZE: 1.5 miles

BANKING IN CORNERS: 15°

DATE BUILT: 2001

FIRST CUP RACE: 2001

SEATING CAPACITY: 80,000

EVENT: Banquet 400 presented by ConAgra Foods

LAS VEGAS MOTOR SPEEDWAY

Las Vegas, Nev.

TYPE: Tri-oval

SIZE: 1.5 miles

BANKING IN CORNERS: 12°

DATE BUILT: 1995

FIRST CUP RACE: 1998

SEATING CAPACITY: 126,000

EVENT: UAW-DaimlerChrysler 400

LOWE'S MOTOR SPEEDWAY

Concord, N.C.

TYPE: Quad-oval

SIZE: 1.5 miles

BANKING IN CORNERS: 24°

DATE BUILT: 1959

FIRST CUP RACE: 1972

SEATING CAPACITY: 167,000

EVENTS: Nextel Open, NASCAR Nextel All-Star Challenge, Coca-Cola 600, Bank of America 500

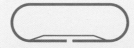

NEW HAMPSHIRE INTERNATIONAL SPEEDWAY

Loudon, N.H.

TYPE: Oval

SIZE: 1.058 miles

BANKING IN CORNERS: 18°

DATE BUILT: 1968

FIRST CUP RACE: 1972

SEATING CAPACITY: 91,000

EVENTS: New England 300, Sylvania 300

RICHMOND INTERNATIONAL RACEWAY

Richmond, Va.

TYPE: Oval

SIZE: 0.75 miles

BANKING IN CORNERS: 14°

DATE BUILT: 1946

FIRST CUP RACE: 1972

SEATING CAPACITY: 105,000

EVENTS: Crown Royal 400, Chevy Rock & Roll 400

WATKINS GLEN INTERNATIONAL

Watkins Glen, N.Y.

TYPE: Road course

SIZE: 2.45 miles

BANKING IN CORNERS: varies

DATE BUILT: 1949

FIRST CUP RACE: 1986

SEATING CAPACITY: varies

EVENT: TBA

MARTINSVILLE SPEEDWAY

Martinsville, Va.

TYPE: Oval

SIZE: 0.526 miles

BANKING IN CORNERS: 12°

DATE BUILT: 1947

FIRST CUP RACE: 1972

SEATING CAPACITY: 86,000

EVENTS: DirecTV 500, Subway 500

PHOENIX INTERNATIONAL RACEWAY

Avondale, Ariz.

TYPE: Oval

SIZE: 1 mile

BANKING IN CORNERS: 11°

DATE BUILT: 1964

FIRST CUP RACE: 1988

SEATING CAPACITY: 100,000

EVENTS: Subway Fresh 500, Checker Auto Parts 500

TALLADEGA SUPERSPEEDWAY

Talladega, Ala.

TYPE: Tri-oval

SIZE: 2.66 miles

BANKING IN CORNERS: 33°

DATE BUILT: 1969

FIRST CUP RACE: 1972

SEATING CAPACITY: 143,000

EVENTS: Aaron's 499, UAW-Ford 500

MICHIGAN INTERNATIONAL SPEEDWAY

Brooklyn, Mich.

TYPE: Tri-oval

SIZE: 2 miles

BANKING IN CORNERS: 18°

DATE BUILT: 1968

FIRST CUP RACE: 1972

SEATING CAPACITY: 82,000

EVENTS: 3M Performance 400 presented by Post-it Picture Paper, GFS Marketplace 400

POCONO RACEWAY

Long Pond, Pa.

TYPE: Tri-oval

SIZE: 2.5 miles

BANKING IN CORNERS: 14°

DATE BUILT: 1968

FIRST CUP RACE: 1974

SEATING CAPACITY: 70,000

EVENTS: Pocono 500, Pennsylvania 500

TEXAS MOTOR SPEEDWAY

Fort Worth, Tex.

TYPE: Quad-oval

SIZE: 1.5 miles

BANKING IN CORNERS: 24°

DATE BUILT: 1997

FIRST CUP RACE: 1997

SEATING CAPACITY: 155,000

EVENTS: Samsung/Radio Shack 500, Dickies 500

The event(s) listed for each track are Nextel Cup races for the 2006 schedule. Note that some events, such as the Budweiser Shootout at Daytona International Speedway and the All-Star Challenge at Lowe's Motor Speedway, involve Cup cars but do not count in the points standings.

NEXTEL CUP SEASON

Race	Race/Track	Date	Top Five — Race	Top Five — Points	
Race 1	Daytona 500 — Daytona International Speedway	02/20/05	Jeff Gordon	Jeff Gordon	185
			Kurt Busch	Kurt Busch	170
			Dale Earnhardt Jr.	Dale Earnhardt Jr.	170
			Scott Riggs	Scott Riggs	160
			Jimmie Johnson	Jimmie Johnson	160
Race 2	Auto Club 500 — California Speedway	02/27/05	Greg Biffle	Kurt Busch	340
			Jimmie Johnson	Jimmie Johnson	335
			Kurt Busch	Mark Martin	301
			Jamie McMurray	Carl Edwards	287
			Carl Edwards	Greg Biffle	273
Race 3	UAW-DaimlerChrysler 400 — Las Vegas Motor Speedway	03/13/05	Jimmie Johnson	Jimmie Johnson	525
			Kyle Busch	Kurt Busch	510
			Kurt Busch	Greg Biffle	428
			Jeff Gordon	Jeff Gordon	418
			Kevin Harvick	Carl Edwards	408
Race 4	Golden Corral 500 — Atlanta Motor Speedway	03/20/05	Carl Edwards	Jimmie Johnson	680
			Jimmie Johnson	Greg Biffle	598
			Greg Biffle	Carl Edwards	593
			Mark Martin	Kurt Busch	577
			Kasey Kahne	Mark Martin	539
Race 5	Food City 500 — Bristol Motor Speedway	04/03/05	Kevin Harvick	Jimmie Johnson	835
			Elliott Sadler	Greg Biffle	741
			Tony Stewart	Tony Stewart	679
			Dale Earnhardt Jr.	Carl Edwards	678
			Dale Jarrett	Elliott Sadlet	657
Race 6	Advance Auto Parts 500 — Martinsville Speedway	04/10/05	Jeff Gordon	Jimmie Johnson	977
			Kasey Kahne	Greg Biffle	817
			Mark Martin	Elliott Sadler	795
			Ryan Newman	Mark Martin	779
			Rusty Wallace	Tony Stewart	774
Race 7	Samsung/Radio Shack 500 — Texas Motor Speedway	04/17/05	Greg Biffle	Jimmie Johnson	1142
			Jamie McMurray	Greg Biffle	1007
			Jimmie Johnson	Rusty Wallace	905
			Casey Mears	Kurt Busch	897
			Sterling Marlin	Jeff Gordon	895
Race 8	Subway Fresh 500 — Phoenix International Raceway	04/23/05	Kurt Busch	Jimmie Johnson	1260
			Michael Waltrip	Kurt Busch	1087
			Jeff Burton	Greg Biffle	1052
			Dale Earnhardt Jr.	Jeff Gordon	1027
			Brian Vickers	Elliott Sadler	1009
Race 9	Aaron's 499 — Talladega Superspeedway	05/01/05	Jeff Gordon	Jimmie Johnson	1368
			Tony Stewart	Kurt Busch	1238
			Michael Waltrip	Jeff Gordon	1217
			Jeremy Mayfield	Greg Biffle	1181
			Jamie McMurray	Elliott Sadler	1164

Race	Race/Track	Date	Top Five — Race	Top Five — Points	
Race 10	Dodge Charger 500 — Darlington Raceway	05/07/05	Greg Biffle	Jimmie Johnson	1519
			Jeff Gordon	Jeff Gordon	1392
			Kasey Kahne	Greg Biffle	1371
			Mark Martin	Kurt Busch	1290
			Ryan Newman	Elliott Sadler	1267
Race 11	Chevy American Revolution 400 — Richmond International Raceway	05/14/05	Kasey Kahne	Jimmie Johnson	1562
			Tony Stewart	Greg Biffle	1521
			Ryan Newman	Jeff Gordon	1438
			Kyle Busch	Elliott Sadler	1413
			Kevin Harvick	Kurt Busch	1407
Race 12	Coca-Cola 600 — Lowe's Motor Speedway	05/29/05	Jimmie Johnson	Jimmie Johnson	1747
			Bobby Labonte	Greg Biffle	1676
			Carl Edwards	Elliott Sadler	1542
			Jeremy Mayfield	Ryan Newman	1530
			Ryan Newman	Jeff Gordon	1516
Race 13	MBNA RacePoints 400 — Dover International Speedway	06/05/05	Greg Biffle	Jimmie Johnson	1912
			Kyle Busch	Greg Biffle	1866
			Mark Martin	Elliott Sadler	1681
			Jimmie Johnson	Ryan Newman	1672
			Rusty Wallace	Tony Stewart	1606
Race 14	Pocono 500 — Pocono Raceway	06/12/05	Carl Edwards	Jimmie Johnson	2062
			Brian Vickers	Greg Biffle	1939
			Joe Nemechek	Elliott Sadler	1781
			Kyle Busch	Carl Edwards	1759
			Michael Waltrip	Mark Martin	1734
Race 15	Batman Begins 400 — Michigan International Speedway	06/19/05	Greg Biffle	Jimmie Johnson	2173
			Tony Stewart	Greg Biffle	2124
			Mark Martin	Elliott Sadler	1923
			Matt Kenseth	Carl Edwards	1914
			Carl Edwards	Mark Martin	1904
Race 16	Dodge/Save Mart 350 — Infineon Raceway	06/26/05	Tony Stewart	Greg Biffle	2250
			Ricky Rudd	Jimmie Johnson	2228
			Kurt Busch	Elliott Sadler	2073
			Rusty Wallace	Tony Stewart	2053
			Dale Jarrett	Mark Martin	2022
Race 17	Pepsi 400 — Daytona International Speedway	07/02/05	Tony Stewart	Jimmie Johnson	2378
			Jamie McMurray	Greg Biffle	2305
			Dale Earnhardt Jr.	Tony Stewart	2242
			Rusty Wallace	Elliott Sadler	2178
			Dale Jarrett	Rusty Wallace	2173
Race 18	USG Sheetrock 400 — Chicagoland Speedway	07/10/05	Dale Earnhardt Jr.	Jimmie Johnson	2548
			Matt Kenseth	Greg Biffle	2440
			Jimmie Johnson	Tony Stewart	2397
			Brian Vickers	Rusty Wallace	2300
			Tony Stewart	Elliott Sadler	2230

Race/Track	Date	Race	Points	
Race 19 New England 300 New Hampshire International Speedway	07/17/05	Tony Stewart	Jimmie Johnson	2672
		Kurt Busch	Greg Biffle	2595
		Bobby Labonte	Tony Stewart	2578
		Kyle Busch	Rusty Wallace	2442
		Greg Biffle	Kurt Busch	2347
Race 20 Pennsylvania 500 Pocono Raceway	07/24/05	Kurt Busch	Jimmie Johnson	2799
		Rusty Wallace	Tony Stewart	2733
		Mark Martin	Greg Biffle	2712
		Carl Edwards	Rusty Wallace	2617
		Ryan Newman	Kurt Busch	2537
Race 21 Allstate 400 at the Brickyard Indianapolis Motor Speedway	08/07/05	Tony Stewart	Tony Stewart	2923
		Kasey Kahne	Jimmie Johnson	2848
		Brian Vickers	Greg Biffle	2812
		Jeremy Mayfield	Rusty Wallace	2705
		Matt Kenseth	Kurt Busch	2646
Race 22 Sirius Satellite Radio at the Glen Watkins Glen International	08/14/05	Tony Stewart	Tony Stewart	3113
		Robby Gordon	Jimmie Johnson	3008
		Boris Said	Greg Biffle	2861
		Scott Pruett	Rusty Wallace	2855
		Jimmie Johnson	Mark Martin	2782
Race 23 GFS Marketplace 400 Michigan International Speedway	08/21/05	Jeremy Mayfield	Tony Stewart	3268
		Scott Riggs	Jimmie Johnson	3142
		Matt Kenseth	Greg Biffle	3016
		Carl Edwards	Rusty Wallace	2979
		Tony Stewart	Mark Martin	2899
Race 24 Sharpie 500 Bristol Motor Speedway	08/27/05	Matt Kenseth	Tony Stewart	3410
		Jeff Burton	Jimmie Johnson	3197
		Greg Biffle	Greg Biffle	3186
		Ricky Rudd	Rusty Wallace	3139
		Rusty Wallace	Mark Martin	3014
Race 25 Sony HD 500 California Speedway	09/04/05	Kyle Busch	Tony Stewart	3570
		Greg Biffle	Greg Biffle	3361
		Brian Vickers	Jimmie Johnson	3312
		Carl Edwards	Rusty Wallace	3257
		Tony Stewart	Mark Martin	3149
Race 26 Chevy Rock & Roll 400 Richmond International Raceway	09/10/05	Kurt Busch	Tony Stewart	3716
		Matt Kenseth	Greg Biffle	3531
		Greg Biffle	Rusty Wallace	3412
		Kyle Busch	Jimmie Johnson	3400
		Rusty Wallace	Kurt Busch	3304
Race 27 Sylvania 300 New Hampshire International Speedway	09/18/05	Ryan Newman	Tony Stewart	5230
		Tony Stewart	Greg Biffle	5210
		Matt Kenseth	Ryan Newman	5190
		Greg Biffle	Rusty Wallace	5190
		Dale Earnhardt Jr.	Matt Kenseth	5180

Race/Track	Date	Race	Points	
Race 28 MBNA RacePoints 400 Dover International Speedway	09/25/05	Jimmie Johnson	Jimmie Johnson	5362
		Kyle Busch	Rusty Wallace	5355
		Rusty Wallace	Ryan Newman	5350
		Mark Martin	Mark Martin	5341
		Ryan Newman	Tony Stewart	5339
Race 29 UAW-Ford 500 Talladega Superspeedway	10/02/05	Dale Jarrett	Tony Stewart	5519
		Tony Stewart	Ryan Newman	5515
		Matt Kenseth	Rusty Wallace	5443
		Ryan Newman	Jimmie Johnson	5437
		Carl Edwards	Greg Biffle	5421
Race 30 Banquet 400 presented by ConAgra Foods Kansas Speedway	10/09/05	Mark Martin	Tony Stewart	5684
		Greg Biffle	Ryan Newman	5609
		Carl Edwards	Greg Biffle	5596
		Tony Stewart	Rusty Wallace	5594
		Matt Kenseth	Jimmie Johnson	5592
Race 31 UAW-GM Quality 500 Lowe's Motor Speedway	10/15/05	Jimmie Johnson	Tony Stewart	5777
		Kurt Busch	Jimmie Johnson	5777
		Greg Biffle	Greg Biffle	5766
		Joe Nemechek	Ryan Newman	5760
		Mark Martin	Mark Martin	5726
Race 32 Subway 500 Martinsville Speedway	10/23/05	Jeff Gordon	Tony Stewart	5957
		Tony Stewart	Jimmie Johnson	5942
		Jimmie Johnson	Ryan Newman	5894
		Bobby Labonte	Greg Biffle	5874
		Jeff Burton	Carl Edwards	5808
Race 33 Bass Pro Shops MBNA 500 Atlanta Motor Speedway	10/30/05	Carl Edwards	Tony Stewart	6100
		Jeff Gordon	Jimmie Johnson	6057
		Mark Martin	Greg Biffle	6025
		Dale Earnhardt Jr.	Carl Edwards	5993
		Matt Kenseth	Ryan Newman	5957
Race 34 Dickies 500 Texas Motor Speedway	11/06/05	Carl Edwards	Tony Stewart	6255
		Mark Martin	Jimmie Johnson	6217
		Matt Kenseth	Carl Edwards	6178
		Casey Mears	Greg Biffle	6133
		Jimmie Johnson	Mark Martin	6132
Race 35 Checker Auto Parts 500 Phoenix International Raceway	11/13/05	Kyle Busch	Tony Stewart	6415
		Greg Biffle	Jimmie Johnson	6363
		Jeff Gordon	Carl Edwards	6328
		Tony Stewart	Greg Biffle	6313
		Bobby Labonte	Mark Martin	6253
Race 36 Ford 400 Homestead-Miami Speedway	11/20/05	Greg Biffle	Tony Stewart	6533
		Mark Martin	Greg Biffle	6498
		Matt Kenseth	Carl Edwards	6498
		Carl Edwards	Mark Martin	6428
		Casey Mears	Jimmie Johnson	6406

Dates and statistics are for 2005.

STAGING A RACE

The stands may be empty, but there are lots of fans during the Samsung/Radio Shack 500 practice at Texas in April 2006.

Well, you've got your tickets, got the car parked. In your carryall bag you've got your sunscreen, program, scanner and some goodies to munch on. You're ready to cheer on your favorite driver and display your loyalty with a hat and shirt with your driver emblazoned on them.

After the race, when the fuel and tire fumes have been blown away into the next county, you take out your earplugs and start back to your car. Great race as usual, you say to yourself, can't wait to come back.

As you're heading down the highway with your head full of the color and excitement that took place in the afternoon, an army of workers is still at the track. They're making sure

your next visit will be as pleasant and memorable as the one you just experienced.

Running a NASCAR Cup race is a monumental task. Sure, there's the actual race Sunday afternoon, but it takes weeks and months to get the facility ready for the onslaught of fans.

Preparations must be made well in advance and with precision timing. In essence a race facility must play host to a gathering of enough people to fill a fair-sized city.

Let's look at it this way: When Lowe's Motor Speedway in Charlotte, North Carolina, hosts the Coca-Cola 600, the Speedway becomes the state's fourth-largest city behind Charlotte, Raleigh and Greensboro. Almost 180,000

people are on the 2,000-acre facility, and they all want to eat, drink, find a place to park and be entertained.

So when these 180,000 people are on their way home, the 400 tons of trash from almost 7,000 trash cans have to be cleaned up. The aisles and halls of the grandstands must be cleaned up. The 113 suites must be cleaned and tidied. And the 1,900 toilets must be attended to.

"Preparing for a race takes a lot of work from many talented people," says Roger Slack, Director of Events for Lowe's Motor Speedway. "It's a huge coordinated effort to bring our fans the best in racing."

Let's start with getting your ticket. You go on line, find the seats of your choice, fill in the electronic form and provide the charge card information. Then in a few days you receive your tickets in the mail.

But there's a huge lead time of over a year for the ticket-process to take place.

"As far as preparation time for tickets, we actually start on the next year's events prior to the current year's event taking place," according to Lowe's Phylis Lipford, who is Director of Ticket Services. "We build our events into the software program, establish our prices and renew current seat holders into the next year's events. Tickets for Ticketmaster outlets and on-line sales are established for the next year right after the current year's event is over."

Fans at Homestead for the Ford 400, the last race of the NASCAR season.

Minor track maintenance at Lowe's. A good track crew knows its surface as well as a pit crew knows its race car.

Lipford added that tickets to be sold at the gate entrances for the event are printed a couple of days prior to the event, and she lines up gate sellers to handle this traffic at least a month before a race.

Lipford works with 11 full-time staff members in ticket sales for Lowe's three Nextel Cup events, Busch Series events and Craftsman Truck Series race. But the number increases to 20 for race weekends, with up to 60 people handling ticket duties at the gates.

Between events, grounds crews use more than 35 tractors and 21 lawn mowers to keep the facility looking well groomed, at a cost of $800,000. And there are 160 flagpoles on the grounds to attend to. And all the lights in the 1,200-fixture permanent lighting system for night racing, installed in 1992 in this first modern superspeedway to implement the Musco system, have to be checked.

So you can now start to appreciate the efforts of 6,000 people working an estimated 100,000 hours to host an event such as the UAW-GM Quality 500.

The media are an integral part of any Cup race, and to help them get the story out to the public, scores of track people work with the media to provide as much information as quickly as possible.

"We credential about 1,200 media members for the Coca-Cola 600, our premier NASCAR event," says Scott Cooper, Director of Marketing and Public Relations at Lowe's. He adds that about 200 of this number are the television broadcast crew.

And how many television cameras are scattered around the track on race day?

"I'm not sure exactly," Cooper replied. "But between the network broadcast and all the local coverage, I'd say about 75 television cameras are on the grounds for race day."

Safety is paramount at any race, but for a race of the scope of a Cup event, every possible contingency is looked after with highly qualified personnel.

Lowe's Emergency Services Director, Norrie Baird, said for a regular race day there are five tow trucks, and three rollback trucks on site for the track area alone. Along with this, there are seven ambulances, five fire trucks and two rescue trucks present at all times.

For the nearly 180,000 people at the track,

emergency and medical services rival those of a mid-sized city.

Along with 18 ambulances and 10 mini-ambulances, there are three first-aid stations on the grounds, each attended by a registered nurse and two paramedics.

In certain areas at Lowe's, such as the VIP suites, the Club and Smith towers, and the grandstands themselves, there are 14 paramedics during race day.

Medical services for drivers, team members and track workers include an outfield care center with a doctor, two registered nurses and three paramedics; and the infield care center with two doctors, two registered nurses and four paramedics.

And there's the always-ready helicopter with flight crew at the infield care center, Baird added.

For actual track preparation and maintenance, three track restoration trucks, one vacuum truck, a fence repair truck, one wall repair truck, two blower tractors, and six jet trucks to dry the surface are all staffed and ready for each race.

And in case of fire, 70 firefighters are stationed with equipment on pit road, at the fuel pumps and in the garage areas.

Fire crews are also spread about the 2,000-acre facility. The track's infield contains one engine company, two brush trucks and a quick response vehicle. Around the property are four engine companies, a ladder truck, two more brush trucks, one squad and two support vehicles. On the roof of the Smith Tower and the Diamond Tower, eight firefighters are ready to respond.

Designed and built in 1959 by O. Bruton Smith and the late Curtis Turner, the 1.5-mile facility has seen a great deal of expansion and improvement over the years in a commitment to customer satisfaction,

And through the efforts of Humpy Wheeler and his staff, Lowe's now has grown to be one of the premier racing facilities on the NASCAR circuit, and has a strong impact on the economy of the area.

"Based on economic impact studies produced

FEEDING THE FANS

With at least 60,000 fans attending a Cup race, literally truck-loads of food and beverages are brought in for the event. And, as can be imagined, enough is brought in to supply what amounts to a small city.

Some fans bring in their own food and drink. And those who camp out on the grounds in their motorhomes are self-sufficient. But for the majority of hungry and thirsty fans in the stands and private suites, track management supplies everything – from hot dogs to ribs and a full range of beverages.

During the running of the Brickyard 400 at Indianapolis Motor Speedway, you can get a Brickyard Burger for $4. An Indy Dog will cost you $3. Some pizza at the Brickyard will cost $6, as will a deli, grilled chicken, Italian sausage, or Philly cheese steak sandwich. The barbecued ribs are the priciest item on the menu at $7.50.

To wash down your meal, a bottle of water will set you back $3, as will a container of ice tea, lemonade or milk. Regular coffee is available in $1 and $3 sizes, or you can get a cappuccino for $3. A can of beer is $4, and mixed drinks such as a Margarita or Bloody Mary, or a Crown Royal will cost $5 or $6.

If you're at the track early, you can get everything to help wake you up, from a $3 blueberry muffin to a $4 cinnamon roll to a regular bacon-and-eggs entrée for $6. And for something to munch on while you're cheering on your heroes, a bag of chips will cost a dollar, a corn-on-the-cob $3, and ice cream treats $3 to $4.

Talladega is the biggest race track on the Cup circuit, at 2.66 miles in length. If the 12,000 pounds of hot dogs served during an event were laid end-to-end on the oval, they would cover the track 1.14 times.

And to wash down these hot dogs and the other available foods, 9,000 gallons of Pepsi alone are consumed at the Alabama track.

by the University of North Carolina at Charlotte, Lowe's Motor Speedway generates an economic impact of more than $400 million on the surrounding three counties," according to Cooper.

"On the whole," Cooper continued, "the entire motorsports industry, which includes NASCAR teams and events, and related businesses, generates a $5.5 billion impact on the state of North Carolina, according to the North Carolina Motorsports Association."

TOP TEAMS

RICHARD CHILDRESS RACING

OWNER:
Richard Childress

CUP DRIVERS:
Kevin Harvick
(No. 29)
Jeff Burton (31)
Clint Bowyer (07)

CREW CHIEFS:
Todd Berrier
(Harvick)
Scott Miller
(Burton)
Gil Martin (Bowyer)

FIRST SEASON: 1969

CAREER CUP WINS:
77

Richard Childress isn't one to sit around and wait for bad to become worse, or for average to become bad.

So, after a mediocre 2005 followed the winless 2004 season – RCR's first shutout since 1997 – Childress made sweeping changes in his company's engine department, and promoted hot Clint Bowyer to a full-time Nextel Cup ride for 2006.

"I'm very encouraged by all the moves Richard has made," said Kevin Harvick, the company's marquee driver.

Harvick was openly dissatisfied with the performance of the Childress cars in 2005 and as 2006 opened, there was still talk he would leave the company if things didn't improve.

Harvick's 14th-place finish was the best of the three RCR drivers in 2005, as Jeff Burton finished 18th in his first year with the team, a drop of six spots from his final year at Roush Racing, and his worst overall placing in a decade. Dave Blaney was 26th, but has been replaced by Bowyer, who finished second in the Busch Series standings for RCR.

The Childress name has been a mainstay around NASCAR tracks for nearly four decades. Childress was a racer himself, making 285 starts, most of them in the team's trademark No. 3 car, which he passed to his close friend Dale Earnhardt in the middle of the 1981 season.

Earnhardt raced elsewhere for 1982 and

1983, but Ricky Rudd filled in admirably, capturing RCR's first pole in his first year, and first victory (Riverside) in his second.

Earnhardt returned in 1984, and over the next 17 years he made the car the most recognizable NASCAR vehicle of its time, winning six Winston Cup drivers' titles. Trading on the popularity of the car and its driver, Childress became the first owner to stylize a car's number, which turned into a marketing bonanza for the company.

But tragedy struck in February 2001. Earnhardt was killed on the final turn of the Daytona 500. A week later, the number was changed to 29, the colors were redone and Harvick was promoted from the Busch Series to

take over the ride. He went on to win rookie of the year.

By then, RCR had become a two-car Cup team, and a third team was added in 2002.

Meanwhile, Childress entered the Craftsman Truck Series in its inaugural year of 1995 and won the first drivers' championship, with Mike Skinner at the wheel. Two years later, Skinner was the founding driver of the second full-time RCR Cup team.

Childress expanded into Busch racing with Harvick and Mike Dillon, his son-in-law. When Harvick won the 2001 Busch Series title, doing double-duty as Earnhardt's Cup replacement, it made Childress the first owner to win a title in each of NASCAR's national divisions.

Kevin Harvick, Richard Childress, DeLana Harvick and Rusty Wallace are all smiles before the Sylvania 300 at New Hampshire, September 2005.

Opposite: Kevin Harvick pits the No. 29 Chevrolet during the Rock & Roll 400 at Richmond, September 2005.

DALE EARNHARDT INC.

OWNER:
Teresa Earnhardt

CUP DRIVERS:
Martin Truex Jr. (No. 1)
Dale Earnhardt Jr. (8)

CREW CHIEFS:
Kevin Manion (Truex Jr.)
Tony Eury Jr. (Earnhardt Jr.)

FIRST SEASON: 1996

CAREER CUP WINS:
22

A NASCAR icon, Dale Earnhardt at the Napa Auto Parts 500 in Fontana, April 2000.

The business of racing is like a car itself. Sometimes it fires on all cylinders and sometimes it needs lots of bodywork.

"It feels like the gears are meshing again," Dale Earnhardt Jr. said of the company Dale Sr. and Teresa Earnhardt founded in 1996.

"There's been a lot of gray areas at DEI for four or five years. We've made some mistakes."

Late in a 2005 season that was riddled with turmoil and bad results, Dale Earnhardt Inc. began to make changes for the future. Some of those changes included undoing previous alterations. With 10 races to go, Earnhardt Jr.'s cousin Tony Eury Jr. was switched back to the No. 8 from Michael Waltrip's car, so the two Juniors could work together again.

Saddled with underperforming cars and sometimes feuding with Waltrip, who was his father's close friend, Earnhardt Jr. had his worst season since becoming a full-time Cup driver in 2000. He won just once, and finished an uncomfortable 19th in the points standings. He had a third place at the Daytona 500, but otherwise did not even fare well in DEI's favorite playgrounds: the restrictor plate tracks. Crew chief

Pete Rondeau lasted only through May and was replaced by Steve Hmiel, the DEI technical director, before Eury Jr. took the reins.

Waltrip, on the way to a disappointing 25th-place standing, was leaving for Bill Davis Racing at the end of the 2005 season anyway, and moving Eury back to the No. 8 was a great way to get a head start on the next season.

Although there were pointed questions during the frustrating racing season, Earnhardt Jr. reaffirmed his loyalty to DEI. The company has stepped up its engine program, and promoted a third Junior to the Cup ranks by giving two-time Busch Series winner Martin Truex Jr. a full-time ride in the No. 1 car.

DEI was founded by Dale Earnhardt, although he never raced for his own company. He neither pushed nor discouraged sons Kerry and Dale Jr. to enter stock car racing, but when they both showed a keen interest, it spurred Dale Sr. and Teresa to establish a team. They ran a limited schedule for the first three years with Robbie Gordon, Steve Park and Darrell Waltrip running a few races. Park became DEI's first full-time driver in 1999, with Earnhardt Jr. racing five times that season and taking over

the second company car the next year.

Earnhardt Jr. won his – and the team's – first race at Texas in April 2000, won again at Richmond, and Park also won a race, giving DEI a huge wave of momentum. They won at least three races every year until the sluggish 2005 season.

In 2001 the operation increased to three cars when Earnhardt Sr. hired Waltrip, who hadn't won in 462 races. Waltrip rewarded his friend's faith with a victory in the Daytona 500, with Earnhardt Jr. second. That, tragically, was the same race in which the company founder was killed.

All four of Waltrip's victories with DEI came at either Daytona or Talladega, where restrictor plate rules are in effect. Earnhardt Jr. has won six times at those tracks.

DEI headquarters attract a lot of tourist traffic because of the company's success, Earnhardt Jr.'s marketability and loyalty to Earnhardt, which still runs strong in the NASCAR heartland. Sitting on 14 acres in Mooresville, North Carolina, and occupying 200,000 square feet of working space, the operation is often called "Garage Mahal."

Three Dales. Dale Earnhardt Jr. (left) with Dad and Dale Jarrett at Daytona in 2000.

Left: Continuing the legacy, Dale Earnhardt Jr. helps celebrate his 2004 Daytona 500 win with step-mom Teresa Earnhardt.

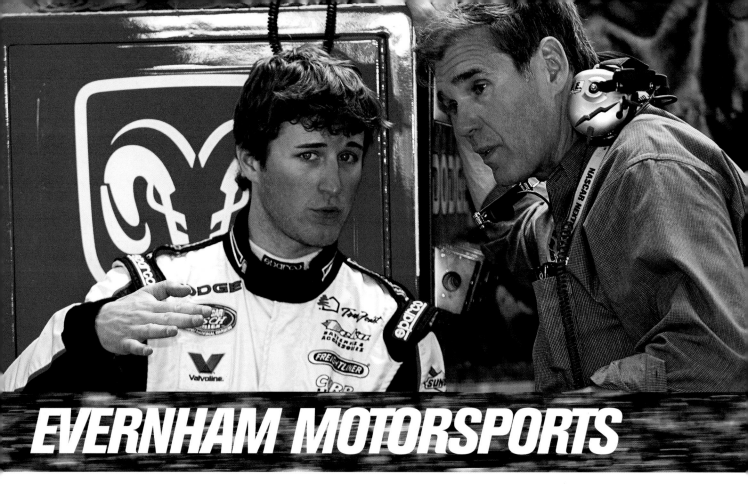

EVERNHAM MOTORSPORTS

OWNER:
Ray Evernham

CUP DRIVERS:
Kasey Kahne
(No. 9)
Scott Riggs (10)
Jeremy Mayfield
(19)

TEAM DIRECTORS:
Kenny Francis
(Kahne)
Rodney Childress
(Riggs)
Chris Andrews
(Mayfield)

FIRST SEASON: 2000

CAREER CUP WINS:
7

Kasey Kahne (left), driver of the No. 9 Evernham Motorsports Dodge, and team owner Ray Evernham chat during practice for the UAW-DaimlerChrysler 400 at Las Vegas, March 2005.

Ray Evernham is not afraid of change – or of taking a chance.

The man who was known as "the crew chief of the 1990s" gambled on leaving Hendrick Motorsports, where he had won 45 Cup races and three Cup drivers' titles overseeing Jeff Gordon's biggest years.

He started his own racing team in 1999, and ventured into a partnership with Dodge, a manufacturer that had been absent from Cup racing for nearly 23 years. And he has decided to take a completely different approach to the way Cup racing crews are organized.

After the Dodges struggled throughout the 2005 season, with only two wins for Evernham (Jeremy Mayfield and Kasey Kahne), he restructured his racing operation. Evernham Motorsports no longer uses official crew chiefs. Instead, the company has developed a team management program. Each car has a leadership team comprising a team director, a car director and an engineer.

Both of Evernham's crew chiefs – well-known Slugger Labbe and Tony Baldwin Jr. – were leaving the company for other employment

anyway, so it was an opportune time to try something new.

And Evernham figures that the configuration problems that restricted Jeremy Mayfield to ninth place and Kahne to 23rd in 2005 won't be a concern for Dodge teams in the future.

"We just missed it aerodynamically with the new body on this car," Evernham said after the 2005 season. "I don't think it's something that's hidden."

Even though 2005 wasn't the huge breakthrough year either driver had hoped for, Mayfield won at Michigan, and Kahne took the first checkered flag of his career at Richmond, the first season that more than one Evernham driver has won a race.

Although Casey Atwood did race an Evernham car three times in 2000, the original deal with Dodge in October 1999 began a marketing-savvy 500-day countdown to the 2001 Daytona 500 – when the team, and Dodge, would make its full-time debut.

It was a spectacular birth for the team as veteran Bill Elliott won the pole. Later in the year, Elliott gave Evernham his first victory as

an owner in the season's final race at Homestead. He also won at Pocono and Indianapolis in 2002.

By 2004 Elliott was easing into retirement and a semi-advisory role with the team, and Mayfield had risen to the top driver's billing. He qualified for the Chase in its first two years, finishing 10th in 2004 and ninth in 2005.

As well as revamping his crew operations for 2006 and beyond, Evernham also expanded, adding promising driver Scott Riggs to move up to three full-time Cup teams for the first time. And Evernham Motorsports was also developing rising star Erin Crocker in the Truck Series.

"All along, we've been saying that we're building a good organization," Evernham says.

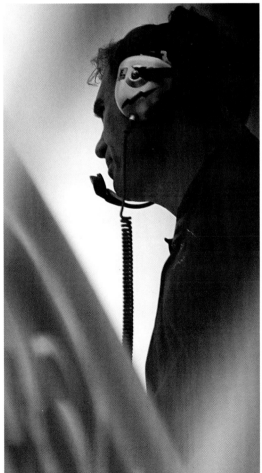

Jeremy Mayfield celebrates after winning the GFS Marketplace 400 at Michigan in August 2005.

Left: Team owner Ray Evernham watches during practice for the Ford 400 at Homestead, November 2005.

JOE GIBBS RACING

OWNER: Joe Gibbs

CUP DRIVERS:
Denny Hamlin (No. 11)
J.J. Yeley (18)
Tony Stewart (20)

CREW CHIEFS:
Mike Ford (Hamlin)
Steve Addington (Yeley)
Greg Zipadelli (Stewart)

FIRST SEASON: 1992

CAREER CUP WINS: 46

Tony Stewart and car chief Jason Shapiro spray owner Joe Gibbs after winning the DirecTV 500 at Martinsville in April 2006.

He's won the Super Bowl of two different sports.

Joe Gibbs returned to the National Football League to coach the Washington Redskins in 2004, and while they have yet to add to the three league titles Gibbs won in his first tenure, Gibbs' racing company took another championship in 2005.

Tony Stewart enjoyed a great summer in 2005, and finished on top of the Nextel Cup drivers' standings, giving Joe Gibbs Racing its third championship in six years.

And, like a successful football franchise that refreshes talent even after a winning year, Joe Gibbs Racing retooled for 2006. Bobby Labonte, who had been with Gibbs since 1995 and gave the company its first driver's championship in 2000, left to join Petty Enterprises.

That left Joe Gibbs Racing with a radically altered hand: a reigning king and two rookie aces. Stewart, who also won the 2002 points championship, went into 2006 with rising star Denny Hamlin and former world outlaw Midget champion J.J. Yeley as teammates.

"Things have changed for me," Stewart said. "I have a responsibility to make sure the other two guys are comfortable where Bobby always made sure I was comfortable."

Hamlin, up from the Busch Series, was comfortable enough that he became the first rookie ever to win the Bud Shootout exhibition race at Dayona in early 2006. With Hamlin's three top-10s and a pole victory in a seven-race Cup debut at the end of 2005, it appeared that Joe Gibbs Racing had found its next racing star.

Gibbs has always had a nose for talent. His first driver was Dale Jarrett, whom he hired soon after he and fellow footballer and stock car fan Don Meredith began putting business plans together for a NASCAR team in 1991. They got important input from Richard Petty and Hendrick Motorsports, leased Hendrick engines and fielded their first team in 1992.

In 1993 Gibbs gave fellow owners an indication of what was to come when Jarrett won the Daytona 500 to open the season, which the veteran coach still calls one his greatest thrills in any sport. Jarrett went on to finish fourth in the points championship.

When Jarrett left for Robert Yates Racing after 1994, Labonte came over from Bill Davis

Racing, where his best finish had been 19th. But in his initial season with JGR, which now had its own engine program, Labonte won the first three races of his career and finished 10th in the points race. He was 11th in 1996, but then began a four-year rise to the top. He finished seventh, sixth and second before finally giving Gibbs his first points championship in 2000.

In 1997, as Labonte was working his way toward the title, Gibbs switched to Pontiacs from Chevrolets, and Gibbs' son J.D. Gibbs took over as president of the racing company. That same year, Gibbs signed Stewart, then a star in open-wheel racing, to a contract for a limited stock car schedule in a joint agreement with Labonte's Busch Series team.

In 1999 Joe Gibbs Racing became a two-car Cup operation with Labonte in No. 18 and Stewart driving the No. 20 car. Stewart won the outside pole for the 1999 Daytona 500, finished fourth overall and was named rookie of the year. He won six races in 2000, but that season belonged to Labonte and his 19 top-five finishes. Labonte won the points title, with Stewart sixth. Stewart was second in 2001 and

took the title in 2002, which counter-balanced an off-year by Labonte, who was 16th.

Stewart and crew chief Greg Zipadelli entered their eighth season together in 2006, with 23 wins as a tandem and a series-leading 248 races together. Joe Gibbs accepted the Redskins' offer to return as president and coach in 2004, but the racing company still ran smoothly under J.D. Gibbs – himself a former football coach – who had joined JGR four months into its first full Cup season.

From 16 employees in its first year of NASCAR involvement, Joe Gibbs Racing has grown into a business employing nearly 400 people.

"We didn't know anything at the start," J.D. Gibbs chuckles, "and that was probably a good thing."

But with three drivers' points titles, it's obvious that they know a lot more now.

Joe Gibbs in the garage during practice for the Coca-Cola 600 at Lowe's in May 2006.

HENDRICK MOTORSPORTS

OWNER: **Rick Hendrick**

CUP DRIVERS:
Jeff Gordon (No. 24)
Jimmie Johnson (48)
Kyle Busch (5)
Brian Vickers (25)

CREW CHIEFS:
Robbie Loomis (Gordon)
Chad Knaus (Johnson)
Alan Gustafson (Busch)
Peter Sospenzo (Vickers)

FIRST SEASON: **1984**

CAREER CUP WINS:
140

Jimmie Johnson congratulates fellow driver Jeff Gordon after Gordon won his third Daytona 500, in February 2005.

There seems to be no tragedy too great for Rick Hendrick to overcome.

The owner of Hendrick Motorsports has had to deal with his own leukemia, which was discovered in 1996 and went into remission three years later, the death of his legendary father "Papa Joe" Hendrick in 2004 and, just a few weeks later, a plane crash near Martinsville, which killed Hendrick's son Ricky and brother John and eight other people closely connected to the company.

And yet his commitment to Nextel Cup racing never wavers. Rather, it usually intensifies.

On the day that John and Ricky (owner of the company's Busch entry) were killed, Hendrick's emerging young star Jimmie Johnson won the race at Martinsville. The very next week, with the entire sport locked in deep grief and Hendrick Motorsport paralyzed by mourning, Johnson won again.

In one of the great organizational achievements in racing history, HMS drivers Johnson and Jeff Gordon finished two–three in the standings in that tragedy-infested 2004 season.

Hendrick Motorsports is the only team to win Cup championships in four consecutive years – 1995, 1996 1997 and 1998.

The team has at least one Cup victory in 20 straight seasons, and in 17 of those years there were three wins or more.

Brian Vickers' Busch Series championship in 2003 gave Hendrick a title in all three of NASCAR's national divisions. Gordon (four) and Labonte (one) have combined for five Cup championships, and truck star Jack Sprague won three in Craftsman Trucks.

But there hasn't been a Cup title since 2001, although Johnson was second twice and was a leading contender until fading to fifth in 2005, and Jeff Gordon was third in 2004. When Gordon sagged to 11th in 2005, Vickers planed out at 17th and Kyle Busch was 20th, despite the first two wins of his promising career, Hendrick took action.

He fine-tuned the organization for the 2006 season and, realizing that you need more drivers in the Chase than the one (Johnson) he had in 2005, Hendrick put up $1.25 million to be divided among all his employees if all four Cup drivers were to qualify for the 10-race playoff. Stock car racing is partly about keeping up with the Joneses, and Roush Racing, with all

five of its drivers in the Chase, were the Joneses of 2005.

"This is the strongest our organization has ever been," Johnson's crew chief Chad Knaus said at the start of the 2006 season. "If we don't make it happen, it's our own fault."

Hendrick has been making it happen since he was 14 and combining with his father, a legend in Modified racing circles, to build his first drag racing car. He eventually constructed a championship boat-racing team before gravitating to NASCAR, where his initial foray wasn't too successful. In 1983, he had hoped to team with country singer Kenny Rogers to put Richard Petty into a Cup car, but the deal fell apart.

Hendrick went at it solo in 1984, with his All Star Racing company, hiring Geoffrey Bodine to drive. On their very first qualifying lap, for the Daytona 500, the engine of the sponsorless car blew out.

"All I wanted that first year was to make the race and hope that I didn't lose everything I had trying to make it work," Hendrick recalls.

It began to work very quickly. Bodine won three times in 1984 and after a winless 1985 season, Hendrick decided to commit to two

full-time Cup teams, bucking the one-car trend of the time. Bodine picked up two wins that year and new teammate Tim Richmond won a stunning seven times.

In the ensuing years, a parade of driving thoroughbreds has passed through the Hendrick stable: Darrell Waltrip, Ricky Rudd, Ken Schrader, Todd Bodine, Ricky Craven, Joe Nemechek – even Al Unser Jr.

But his biggest catch was the one who was slowest to win favor in the sport. In 1993 Hendrick contracted a 21-year-old Californian who was the rising star in open-wheel racing. Gordon was young, urban, not from the traditional belt of NASCAR states, and was untested in stock cars. He had everything going against him but charisma, talent and Hendrick Motorsports. Gordon began collecting Cup checkered flags in his sophomore season and hasn't stopped since.

Running parallel to his racing interests, Hendrick has created one of the United States' largest automotive businesses, with 60 dealerships coast-to-coast, which has enlarged despite his personal burden. It's no wonder his drivers are always so inspired.

Rick Hendrick chats with Jimmie Johnson during the Daytona 500 practice in 2006. This time, Jimmie Johnson was the Hendrick driver who won the event.

PENSKE RACING SOUTH

OWNER:
Roger Penske

CUP DRIVERS:
Kurt Busch (No. 2)
Ryan Newman (12)

CREW CHIEFS:
Roy McCauley
(Busch)
Matt Borland
(Newman)

FIRST SEASON: 1972

CAREER CUP WINS:
57

Ryan Newman
and Roger Penske
celebrate after
winning the Ford
300 Busch event
at Homestead in
November 2005.

"The name is as closely associated with car racing as the wheel." Roger Penske.

And it has the kind of allure that made 2004 Nextel Cup champion Kurt Busch want to jump ship a year early from Roush Racing to join Penske Racing South. That teamed him with another young veteran, Ryan Newman, for the 2006 Nextel Cup season.

Penske South came out of 2005 with just one win, from Newman, as Dodges struggled throughout the entire Cup season. But the addition of Busch to run with Newman, who was sixth in the 2005 drivers' standings, was expected to provide a boost over the next few years. Rusty Wallace, who finished eighth overall but didn't have a win, retired after his 15th season with Penske.

Wallace was the last driver Penske employed before leaving NASCAR to concentrate on open-wheel interests in 1980 and the first one he hired when he returned to stock cars for good in 1991. The team's greatest success came in 1993 when Wallace had 10 victories and was runner-up in the drivers' standings.

Penske made his name in road racing, but made his fortune in the business of racing.

He owns a huge transportation company that includes vehicle leasing, automotive retail and tire sales.

Penske Racing Inc. is the most successful Indy car organization in history and has 11 victories at the Indy 500. Penske has also won nine CART championships, three in the SCCA and two in USRRC.

Penske moved into NASCAR racing in 1972, and got his first win, at Riverside, from former road racer Mark Donohue a year later. He ran only one full season – 1976 when Bobby Allison finished fourth overall – before concentrating solely on open wheel from 1981 to 1990.

With Wallace picking up 37 Cup victories in his 15 years, Penske South became as closely connected to stock car racing as it's always been to open wheel. The organization has never claimed a points championship, but Newman has led in poles three times (2003–05) and wins once (eight in 2003).

After two years with three entries, Penske South cut its complement of Cup cars to two before the 2006 season, but in Busch and Newman they've got a pair of the best, with solid futures ahead of them.

PETTY ENTERPRISES

As veteran Bobby Labonte says of his new employers, "We've got the number, the car, the owners, the name."

But Petty Enterprises, which was there in 1949 for the inaugural season of NASCAR's Grand National Division, which eventually became the Nextel Cup Series, has fallen on hard times lately.

The racing team was founded by the great Lee Petty and has produced four generations of NASCAR drivers, one of the most prolific lineages in all professional sport. Founder Lee Petty won the first Daytona 500 and three drivers' titles, and his son Richard won seven Cup championships.

But in the last 22 years, Petty Enterprises has captured just three Cup races, and none since John Andretti won in 1999.

"We'd made very little progress the last four or five years and we just weren't going in the right direction," said Kyle Petty, who runs the day-to-day operation in addition to driving the No. 45 car. "Things changed. We always did everything in the backyard and we were successful. It's taken time to catch up."

When Petty (27th) and Jeff Green (29th)

managed only two top-10 finishes in 2005, changes had to be made.

Veteran Bobby Labonte moved over from Joe Gibbs Racing and into the No. 43 car made famous by Richard Petty. Todd Parrott, who helped Dale Jarrett to the 1999 championship, was brought in as his crew chief. Petty also hired Jeff Loomis, the crew chief for Jeff Gordon's 2001 championship season, as executive vice-president of operations.

Labonte became the 46th driver Petty Enterprises has fielded cars for. Among the big names who've been behind the wheel are Ralph Earnhardt, Buddy Baker, Bobby Hamilton and Kyle Petty himself, who put his own team under the Petty Enterprises umbrella in 1999.

Petty Enterprises was hit hard by tragedy in 2000 when founder Lee Petty died from surgery complications and Kyle Petty's son Adam was killed during practice for a Busch race at New Hampshire International Speedway.

Kyle Petty and his wife Pattie, who were already deeply involved in charity work, stepped up their commitment even further and in 2004 opened the Victory Junction Gang Camp for ill children.

OWNER:
Richard Petty

CUP DRIVERS:
Bobby Labonte (No. 43)
Kyle Petty (45)

CREW CHIEFS:
Todd Parrott (Labonte)
Paul Andrews (Petty)

FIRST SEASON: 1949

CUP WINS: 268

NASCAR icon Richard Petty signs autographs while his son Kyle waits for the pen. The pits, Pocono, July 2005.

ROUSH RACING

OWNER:
Jack Roush

CUP DRIVERS:
Mark Martin
(No. 6)
Greg Biffle (16)
Matt Kenseth (17)
Jamie McMurray
(26)
Carl Edwards (99)

CREW CHIEFS:
Pat Tryson
(Martin)
Doug Richert
(Biffle)
Robbie Reiser
(Kenseth)
Jimmy Ferris
(McMurray)
Bob Osborne
(Edwards)

FIRST SEASON: 1988

CAREER CUP WINS:
89

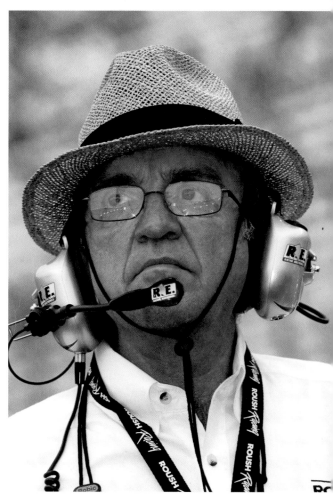

What do you call an owner who captures back-to-back Nextel Cup points championships but has his best year when none of his drivers wins it all? Jack Roush.

Fully one-half of the 10 drivers who qualified for the Chase in 2005 came out of the Roush Racing stable. Although Tony Stewart took the championship for Joe Gibbs, Roush had Greg Biffle in second, relative newcomer Carl Edwards a surprising third, reliable veteran Mark Martin a shocking fourth, former champion Matt Kenseth seventh and volatile Kurt Busch 10th, even though he was suspended for the final two races.

Five. Count 'em, five. Every driver Roush entered was in contention for the 10-race playoff. That domination by Roush and the Fords was probably a major factor in NASCAR proposing to limit the number of cars an owner can enter.

Roush has had tremendous success since 1988 when he moved into NASCAR after two decades in drag racing and sports car racing. But despite multiple victories from Martin, his original driver, and Jeff Burton, Roush didn't win a points championship until 2003, when a very consistent season by Kenseth earned the final Winston Cup title.

The very next year, Roush won again with Kurt Busch topping the drivers' standings. By the middle of 2005, however, Busch was yearning to join Penske South even though his contract had more than a year to run with Roush. The two veteran owners worked out a deal involving third party Chip Ganassi, and Busch was released to join Penske a year early and promising Jamie McMurray was released to join Roush.

Meanwhile, Roush had persuaded Martin, who was halfway through his Salute to You farewell tour, to remain for 2006. In the blink of an eye, Martin said yes to his friend.

Roush, whose trademark is a straw hat, is a creative owner who plans well for the future. His company runs the popular Driver X competition on TV, nicknamed the Gong Show, to pick a driver for Roush's Craftsman Truck entries. Todd Kluever, who won that "Race for the Ride" in 2004, raced Craftsman in 2005 and is slated to take over Martin's No. 6 Nextel Cup ride in 2007.

And Roush, combining with Robert Yates, can build cars.

"The way the front ends are designed, the aerodynamic package they've got, you've got to hand it to Jack Roush," veteran Rusty Wallace has said.

Roush earned a master's degree in scientific mathematics from Eastern Michigan University while he was working at Ford Motor Company. He left Ford in 1969 and started the "Fastbacks," a group that designed and ran drag racers.

When the Fastbacks broke up after two years, Roush joined Chrysler Corporation as an engineer and formed another successful drag racing partnership with Wayne Gapp.

He was also building engines for power boats and oval-track cars and by 1978 had formed Jack Roush Performance Engineering, to solidify the engine-building business. Over the next 14 years he won 24 titles in the Sports Car Club of America and the International Motor Sports Association.

After a modest NASCAR start in 1988 with no wins, and 10 DNFs with Martin, Roush Racing got its first win late in 1989, when Martin crossed the finish line first at Rockingham.

The following year, the one-car team won three races and finished third in the points standings. Martin would run up three more third-place finishes over the next 14 years, and his fourth place in 2005 was the biggest surprise of all. Roush also had third-place finishes out of Burton (2000) and Busch (2002) before Kenseth and Busch won their back-to-back titles.

Roush crashed his plane into a small lake in southern Alabama and, unconscious, was submerged in the lake. A retired marine who witnessed the accident dove into the water, hauled Roush to the surface and resuscitated him.

Within six weeks he got back to the track, and the following year he won his first points championship.

Mark Martin leads Greg Biffle during the Banquet 400 at Kansas in October 2005. Martin started 19th, but went on to win the race. Biffle took second, and Carl Edwards was third.

Opposite top: Jack Roush gets a blast from Greg Biffle during celebrations after Biffle won his third Cup race of 2005 – the Dodge Charger 500 at Darlington.

Opposite bottom: Jack Roush during qualifying for the Sharpie 500 at Bristol in August 2005. Roush driver Matt Kenseth won the race.

WOOD BROTHERS/JTG RACING

OWNERS:
Glen, Len and Eddie Wood, Kim Wood Hall, Tad Geschickter

CUP DRIVER:
Ken Schrader (21)

CREW CHIEF:
David Hyler (Schrader)

FIRST SEASON: 1953

CAREER CUP WINS:
96

As part of one of NASCAR's oldest teams, these Wood Brothers crew members, shown at the Kansas Speedway, carry on a long and respected tradition.

Wood Brothers Racing could set up a racing hall of fame in its garage, inducting no one but former employees.

David Pearson, Cale Yarborough, Marvin Panch, Tiny Lund, Bobby Rahal, Parnelli Jones, A.J. Foyt, Donnie Allison, Buddy Baker, Dale Jarrett, Neil Bonnett, Michael Waltrip, Ricky Rudd. And, now, Ken Schrader.

They've all been behind the wheel of cars owned by the company that was founded in 1953 by driver Glen Wood and his brother Leonard. When Glen Wood retired in 1961 with three Cup race wins to his credit, he became crew chief and Leonard assisted him. But it was Leonard who was recognized as the forefather of the organized pit stop.

The Woods' greatest successes came in 1965 when they pit-crewed Jimmy Clark's victory at the Indy 500; in 1973 when the legendary Pearson won 11 Cup races; and in 1976 when Pearson won 10 times.

Although Wood Brothers Racing has taken nearly 100 Cup races, precious few of them have come in recent years. Elliott Sadler's 2001 victory at Bristol is the company's only victory since 1993.

"We were competitive, we just didn't win a race," Eddie Wood said after the 2005 season, when Rudd finished 21st in the drivers' standings and had two top-fives.

Rudd went into semi-retirement after 2005, and Ken Schrader came over from Robert Yates Racing to drive the No. 21 car. It's still the only full-time Cup car the Woods enter, but before the 2006 season, the Woods formed an alliance with Busch Series owner, Tad Geschickter, who is well-known for his marketing sense.

The combined companies have Schrader – whose last victory was in 1991 – plus a part-time entry in Cup racing, and two entries each in the Busch and Craftsman Truck series.

"Tad helps with funding and I can concentrate on racing," said co-owner Eddie Wood, Glen's son.

Michael "Fatback" McSwain moved up from crew chief to become director of racing.

"Basically we've structured it as a giant leasing company, leasing cars and trucks to five teams," McSwain says. "Everybody works on everything."

ROBERT YATES RACING

It was close, but Robert Yates kept his streak alive.

Since he started his own racing team in 1989, the master engine builder has won at least one Nextel Cup race every season.

In 2005 Robert Yates Racing had to wait until the 29th race of the season, but the team made it 17 straight years, when Dale Jarrett tiptoed through wreckage to win at Talladega.

That victory brought a little sunlight into a fairly stormy season, during which Jarrett's teammate Elliot Sadler didn't win a race, neither car qualified for the Chase and Jarrett had to switch crew chiefs twice.

With Sadler finishing 13th in the drivers' standings and Jarrett two spots lower, Yates joined a host of other owners who made changes to their organization during the winter of 2005–06.

Richard "Slugger" Labbe became the crew chief of Jarrett's No. 88, and another Daytona 500 winner, Tommy Baldwin Jr., took over for Sadler. Additionally, Kevin Buskirk, who had been a Yates crew chief, became technical and performance director and Ed Guzzo came on as production and operational director.

It was all part of Yates' long-term plan to expand into a four-team organization for Nextel Cup racing. For now, the RYR Cup team remains a two-car operation with veteran Jarrett and the improving Sadler, who finished ninth in 2004.

Yates has had two cars in Cup racing since 1996, when Ernie Irvan won two races and Jarrett won four. The team began in 1989 with Davey Allison behind the wheel, and won 15 races until Allison's death in 1993.

Jarrett won the driver's title with a stunning 24 top-five finishes in 1999, Yates' peak season to date, but some pretty good years also followed when Ricky Rudd teamed up with Jarrett. In their three years together, the veterans combined for 11 victories and 71 top-fives. During that stretch Yates contracted United Parcel Service as Jarrett's sponsor.

Yates drove dragsters himself during the 1950s and helped Bobby Allison win the 1983 driver's title before launching his own team for the 1989 season. Davey Allison won twice that year, setting the template for at least one victory per season since then.

OWNER:
Robert Yates

CUP DRIVERS:

Elliott Sadler (No. 38)

Dale Jarrett (88)

CREW CHIEFS:

Tommy Baldwin Jr. (Sadler)

Slugger Labbe (Jarrett)

FIRST SEASON: 1989

CAREER CUP WINS: 57

Top left: Robert Yates and Elliott Sadler during practice at the fabled Brickyard in the Allstate 400, August 2005.

Top right: Dale Jarrett and Elliott Sadler lead the pack at the start of the UAW-Ford 500 at Talladega, October 2005. Jarrett won the race.

TOP DRIVERS

GREG BIFFLE

NO. 16

BORN:
December 23, 1969

HOMETOWN:
Vancouver, Wash.

TEAM:
Roush Racing

CAR: Ford

SPONSOR:
Army National
Guard

CUP WINS: 9

2005 CUP EARNINGS:
$5,729,928

CAREER EARNINGS:
$13 million

When Greg Biffle arrives, he REALLY arrives.

The Washington State native worked his way steadily up NASCAR's developmental ranks, so it took him several years to become an overnight success.

But what a success it was. In 2005, in just his third full season in Nextel Cup, Biffle fell a mere 35 points short of becoming the first driver to win all three of NASCAR's major series.

"I had a lot of time behind the wheel, and I wouldn't really change it for anything," says Biffle, the highest finisher of the five Jack Roush drivers who qualified for the 2005 Chase. "I've learned so much from racing trucks and from the Busch Series. I've learned so much about car control, about pit stops."

With regulations on softer tires and shorter spoilers helping create the looser cars in which Biffle excels, 2005 was a breakthrough year for Biffle, who had finished 20th, with one victory, as a rookie in 2003 and 17th, with two victories, in 2004.

It was one of those 2004 triumphs, in the season finale at Homestead that laid a firm foundation for Biffle's explosion into the limelight in the first half of 2005. While most of the attention at Homestead was on the crowning of the points winner, Biffle's Roush teammate Kurt Busch, the No. 19 car was signaling that it was ready for the next year.

After finishing 25th at Daytona to open 2005, Biffle won the next race at California, and then ran off finishes of sixth, third, ninth, and 29th before winning again at Texas. Three races later, he won again at Darlington and two wins in three weeks at Dover and Michigan gave him five checkered flags and another five top-10 finishes in the season's opening 15 races. By the 10th race, he'd already doubled his career total of three Cup wins.

It seemed that Biffle was poised to add the 2005 Nextel Cup crown to the Craftsman Truck Series championship he won in 2000 and the Busch Series title he won in 2002. But his results flattened out after his mid-June victory at Michigan, and although he added a whopping 10 top-five finishes in the second half of the season, he didn't win another race until the season finale at Homestead. By then he had conceded that he wouldn't win the title, but he came a lot closer than he imagined. He finished among the top three in 13 races and, arguably, only a pair of 20ths two weeks apart during the Chase stood between him and a third national series title.

Biffle's year of coming close also included the 2005 Busch Series, where in his final 10 starts of the year, he didn't win but was runner-up six times.

"I'm the king of second places," he quipped.

Biffle drives hard and fast and doesn't fret about slippage on the corners. Noted for his

Above: Biffle in the pits at Richmond during the Crown Royal 400 in May 2006. He started on the pole and took fourth in the National Guard Ford.

Opposite: Greg Biffle, ready to do battle at Darlington. After starting ninth, the Washington State driver won the May 2006 running of the Dodge Charger 500.

In the traditional tire-burning win ceremony, Biffle celebrates on the track (above), and in Victory Lane (opposite) after winning the 2005 season-ender at Homestead.

"If I'd moved out of those series a year earlier, I wouldn't have had either title."

deft hands and quick feet, he honed his craft at every NASCAR level until he felt he was completely ready for the next move up. As a result, he was older than most of his peers when he broke into the upper levels of stock car racing.

He started his career on the quarter-miles of the Pacific northwest, and in 1994 joined NASCAR's weekly racing series, where he remained for four seasons. He won the Late Model championships at both Washington's TriCity Raceway and Portland. In 1995 he won a stunning 27 times in 43 starts and, just to prove that he was no flash in the pan, he won 27 of 47 races in 1996 when he was runner-up for the Pacific Coast championship.

In 1996, as Biffle was dominating the Late Models Winter Heat Series at Tucson Raceway, a turning point occurred in his career. Former Cup winner Benny Parsons, now a broadcaster, took note of his Tucson performances and recommended Biffle to Jack Roush.

Roush hired him to run Craftsman Trucks in 1997 and all Biffle did was win rookie of the year and set a series rookie record with four poles. In 1999, at Memphis, he won his first NASCAR national series race and went on to

finish second in the points standing and set a Craftsman series record with nine victories. He remained one more year in the Craftsman series and won the title.

Biffle moved up to Busch Grand National in 2001 and turned in one of the best rookie seasons in the series' history, with five wins, two poles and 16 top-five finishes. He won four more races in 2002 and became the first driver to win Busch and Craftsman Truck Series.

"If I'd moved out of those series a year earlier, I wouldn't have had either title," Biffle says.

But after the Busch title, it was time for Roush to promote Biffle to the premier series and early in July 2003, under the lights at Daytona, he won his first Cup race, the Pepsi 400. He went on to finish 20th overall, and second in the rookie-of-the-year standings.

When Biffle moved up only three places in 2004, some observers felt he might not make the impact in Nextel Cup that he had at other levels. Partway through that season he was even talking about leaving Roush Racing. But then he won at Homestead to end the season, which put him right on track for the stunning impact of 2005.

JEFF BURTON

NO. 31

BORN: June 29, 1967

HOMETOWN: South Boston, Va.

TEAM: Richard Childress Racing

CAR: Chevrolet

SPONSOR: Cingular

CUP WINS: 17

2005 CUP EARNINGS: $4,265,666

CAREER EARNINGS: $40 million

The only way to turn bad times into good ones is to learn from them.

Jeff Burton believes in that process, largely because he has to. After a dominating stretch of five seasons from 1997 to 2001, when he won 17 races, compiled 72 top-5 finishes and never finished out of the top 10 in the points race, Burton entered the 2006 season in a four-year winless drought.

After switching to Richard Childress Racing from Jack Roush in August 2004, Burton struggled through a 2005 season that had very few high points and which helped prompt massive changes in almost every department of RCR.

After finishing 18th in the points standing

for the second straight year, Burton admitted that his team hadn't prepared well enough for the ever-changing demands of a Nextel Cup season.

"We have addressed every single part of what makes the cars go fast," Burton said as he entered 2006 with new crew chief Scott Miller, who replaced Kevin Hamlin with two races to go in 2005. That change, part of sweeping adjustments at RCR, was made to get a head start on the following season, Childress said at the time.

Finishing 18th and leading a mere seven laps all year was nothing close to what Burton had in mind when he moved from Roush to Childress with 14 races remaining on the 2004

schedule. Roush had been unable to pick up a major sponsor for Burton in 2004, but the company itself financed the No. 99 car. Burton was grateful for the support, and made sure the public knew about it.

"He's been such a good friend and such a great ambassador for NASCAR, I wasn't going to be the guy who put Jeff Burton on the street," Jack Roush said. And Roush didn't stand in Burton's way when the opportunity to join Childress came along in mid-season. So, after a dozen seasons in Fords, Burton became a Chevy driver.

But while his replacement, Carl Edwards, became an instant celebrity in the No. 99, Burton struggled in the RCR No. 31.

Burton said that "a 17-race winner didn't forget how to win, but maybe the way he was winning doesn't work anymore." He would make adjustments, he said. It was clear that in 2005 Burton had neither the cars nor the momentum to contend, and some experts, including Burton himself, felt it was actually one of his better seasons behind the wheel because he got everything he could out of his equipment.

Racing fans would expect no less out of Burton, given his exemplary history.

Growing up in Virginia with an older brother (Ward) who raced go-karts, Burton caught the kart craze himself and by the time he was 17 had won two state titles and been

Jeff Burton had a good showing in the Aaron's 499 at Talladega in May 2006, placing fourth after starting in 40th spot. A month earlier, the Cingular Chevy driver finished 33rd at Martinsville (above).

Burton gets his Chevy warmed up at the Samsung/Radio Shack 500 in April 2006. He took sixth.

"I knew I was stepping into something that needed a lot of work."

runner-up four times. In 1984 he moved into pure stocks and two years later, at 19, he won six Late Model races at South Boston Speedway. In 1988, he entered five NASCAR Busch Series races, in a car owned by his father John. Following two top-five finishes in 1989, he won his first Busch race in 1990 at Martinsville.

After finishing 12th in the Busch standings in 1991 and 1992, Burton made his Cup debut at New Hampshire, qualifying sixth and finishing 37th. That got Stavola Brothers Racing interested, and he signed with them for 1994, grabbing two top-five finishes. He also beat his brother Ward for the rookie-of-the-year title.

Burton spent one more year with the Stavolas, then moved to Roush Racing in 1996, vaulting to 13th in the points standings from 32nd the year before.

In 1997 he won his first Cup race, in the inaugural premier series race at Texas Motor Speedway, won again at New Hampshire and Martinsville, and finished fourth in the drivers' standings. That was the first of four straight years among the top five.

Burton was fifth in 1998 and 1999, amass-

ing 36 top-five finishes and eight victories, including a series-leading six in 1999. He tied for the most victories in 2000 with four, and finished third in the points race behind Bobby Labonte and Dale Earnhardt. Twice that year, he won races in which his brother Ward was the runner-up.

Burton won twice in 2001, a season in which he also became an advocate for enhanced safety in Cup races after Earnhardt's death in the Daytona 500. But he dropped to 10th in the points standings and his top-10 finishes plunged significantly.

In 2002, for the first time in six years, he didn't win a race and his ranking dropped to 12th. Similar results in 2003, and the spiraling costs of financing a Cup team, led him to open 2004 without a sponsor. Just past the halfway point in the season, he made the move to Childress.

"I knew I was stepping into something that needed a lot of work," Burton said as he entered 2006 with renewed hope. "Last year we were rebuilding, this year we have to perform."

KURT BUSCH

When Kurt Busch won the inaugural Chase for the Nextel Cup in 2004, his on-track motto was "don't get into trouble."

He should have paid attention to that when he was off the track, too.

The ultra-talented driver, one of the large stable of Young Guns who reached NASCAR's top series at the turn of the 21st century, has had his share of successes. And more than his share of trouble.

Busch has such an ability to read races and tracks that owner Jack Roush had him skip the Busch Grand National ranks completely and promoted him to the then-Winston Cup in 2001. He had finished second in Crafts-

man Truck Series the year before, and Roush thought the 22-year-old was ready for The Bigs.

Critics argued that this was too rapid a rise for a young man who had only been racing competitively for eight years, and that he needed to handle himself as well as he handled his cars. And the critics were right. It didn't take long for Busch to establish himself as the driver other drivers loved to hate.

In August 2003, veteran Jimmy Spencer reached into the No. 97 car after the Michigan 400 and punched Busch, whom he accused of running him into a wall. Spencer was fined $25,000 and suspended for a week, but Busch was also fined for unprofessional behavior and lost a great deal of fan support.

NO. 2

BORN:
August 4, 1978

HOMETOWN:
Las Vegas, Nev.

TEAM:
Penske South

CAR: **Dodge**

SPONSOR:
Miller Lite

CUP WINS: **14**

2005 CUP EARNINGS:
$6,516,318

CAREER EARNINGS:
$28 million

Kurt Busch getting the once-over in the pits in the former Rusty Wallace Ford.

In September 2005, on the second lap of the Sylvania 300, the first race of the Chase, Scott Riggs slid into Busch, sending him into the wall and out of the race. Busch soon verbally confronted Riggs' crew chief.

And just before the second-last race of 2005 at Phoenix, Busch was hit with a misdemeanor driving citation by Maricopa County, Arizona, sheriff's deputies. Although early allegations of drinking and driving were later proven false, Busch did admit that he had been belligerent with the deputies.

His owner suspended Busch for the final two races of the season, and of his career at Roush Racing. He had already rocked the NASCAR

world by asking out of his contract to take over Rusty Wallace's famous No. 2 at Penske South. That release was granted, naturally.

The late-season controversies overshadowed what was a strong 2005 for the Las Vegas native. He started the season as runner-up at the Daytona 500, and followed with a pair of third-place finishes, had nine top-five finishes and 18 top-10s, and won three times. But the dream of a repeat championship ended just two laps into the Chase when he was run into the wall. He eventually finished 10th overall.

Busch had avoided such unpleasantness in 2004, when he stayed remarkably consistent and tried to use cautious aggression in most races. He won three times, one fewer than each of the two previous years, but also had only three DNFs, his lowest total in four full years of Cup racing.

Entering the Chase in seventh place, Busch won the Sylvania 300 and moved into first for good with eight races to go. In the final 10 races, he finished out of the top 10 only once and was sixth or better eight times. Still, he won the Nextel Cup title by only eight points over Jimmie Johnson and 16 over third-place Jeff Gordon.

It took steely nerves for him not to panic when his wheel fell off near pit road on the 93rd lap of the 2004 season finale at Homestead. When he got back on the track he was buried in 28th spot, "and it was time to either shape up or ship out." He climbed all the way back to fifth overall. Johnson and Gordon both beat him, but not by enough, and he had his title.

He was always known as a quick learner and a precocious talent. His father Tom, a transplanted Chicagoan, was an auto mechanic, a tool salesman and a prominent driver on Las Vegas short tracks. When he was eight, Busch started to work in his father's garage after school, a practice his younger brother Kyle would also follow.

Busch started serious racing at the age of 14 in Dwarf cars and won the Nevada rookie of the year in 1994, when he was 16. Two years later he was Hobby Stock Champion at Las Vegas Speedway Park and also Legends rookie of the year. Two years after that, he was named rookie of the year in NASCAR's Southwest Touring series. He won the touring title in 1999, when he also successfully auditioned for a ride with Roush in the NASCAR Craftsman Truck Series.

After winning four truck races and finishing runner-up in the 2000 points title, Busch graduated directly to Cup racing. He was runner-up to Kevin Harvick for the 2001 rookie-of-the-year award, finishing 27th overall. Then Roush struck gold when he shifted veteran crew chief Jim Fennig to Busch's car for 2002. By March they had their first Winston Cup victory at Bristol, and they won three of

the last five races on the schedule to finish third overall.

It appeared that a championship might be in the cards for 2003, when Busch won once and was second twice in the first six races, but the cards had other ideas. He suffered blown tires, blown engines, and the problems with Spencer. Despite winning four times, he was 11th in the standings.

Then came his points championship in 2004, and the strong, but incident-plagued, 2005.

"You have to be a good guy and take care of your public image," Busch said, promising to do so at Penske.

Busch did not have a good day at Fort Worth in April 2006. The Miller Lite car placed 34th after starting seventh.

KYLE BUSCH

NO. 5
BORN: May 2, 1985
HOMETOWN:
Mooresville, N.C.
TEAM: Hendrick
Motorsports
CAR: Chevy
SPONSOR: Kellogg's
CUP WINS: 2
2005 CUP EARNINGS:
$4,185,239
CAREER EARNINGS:
$4.5 million

The term "Young Guns" was meant for those – like his brother Kurt – who stormed onto the scene just a few years ahead of him, but Kyle Busch became the youngest gun of them all.

Busch was 20 years, four months and two days old when he held off Greg Biffle under a green-white-checkered finish to take the California 500 in early September 2005. It was the first Nextel Cup victory of what promises to be an exciting career, and nobody had done it any sooner. The previous Cup record for youngest race winner was Dave Thomas, who was four days older than Busch when he won at Atlanta in November 1952.

There must be something about California Speedway: in the season's first race there, Busch had become the youngest pole sitter in Cup history, before dropping off to a 23rd-place finish.

"My nerves were getting to me a bit," Busch admitted after his first career victory. "But that was just unbelievable."

Busch's older brother was waiting in Victory Lane to share in the victory dance. When Kyle Busch proved that his inaugural win was no fluke by doing it again at Phoenix 10 weeks later, it was the first time that brothers had won at the same track in the same season since Donnie and Bobby Allison swept the two races at Atlanta in 1978. But this time, Kurt wasn't

there to celebrate. He had been suspended by Roush Racing earlier that very same day for an off-track incident with local police.

It was that kind of up-and-down year for the talented young speedster who was born in Las Vegas.

In a Nextel Cup season, which included only one other full-time freshman (Travis Kvapil), Busch romped to the 2005 rookie-of-the-year honors, with two victories and an impressive nine top-five finishes, good enough for 20th place in the drivers' standings. The only other time his boss Rick Hendrick had picked up rookie-of-the-year honors was in 1993, when Jeff Gordon topped the first-year class.

But Busch would have finished much higher in 2005, perhaps even qualified for the Chase, had he been able to keep his No. 5 car on the track more often. Eight times he did not finish a race, the second highest number of DNFs among the Nextel Cup's top-20 drivers. And although he's considered mature for such a young driver, completing races is an area in which Busch still has to ripen a bit.

That improvement will come from recognizing when the car just isn't in top-five tune on race day. Instead of pushing an average car too hard by trying to make it a good car, and finishing somewhere lower than 30th, Busch says his plan is to drive the car that's there that day to its full capabilities, but no further. That should result in fewer disastrous finishes.

Running the Kellogg's Chevy of Hendrick Motorsports, the young Busch and former Cup rookie placed 33rd in the Sharpie 500 at Bristol in 2005.

It was in the Nevada Desert that Kyle watched his older brother race Legend Cars with great success, and decided to follow the same path himself, often driving the same cars Kurt had. He began Legends at the age of 13 and won two titles in that division at Las Vegas Motor Speedway. By the time he left Legends, he'd won 65 times.

He graduated to Late Models in 2001 and won 10 races at Las Vegas. And he also made six starts in the NASCAR Craftsman Truck Series for Roush Racing, his brother's employers. Two top-10 finishes in those six races indicated that he indeed had a future in big-time racing, so he accelerated his education and graduated from high school in 2002, a year early.

But by then, NASCAR had instituted its new policy that all participants, including drivers, in its national and Touring series must be 18 or older. Busch was only 17, so he moved to the ASA for a season, finishing eighth overall and third in the rookie standings.

The next year he was eligible for NASCAR, but instead of signing with Roush, Busch joined Hendrick Motorsports in May 2003. In his Busch Series debut, he finished second at Lowe's, then picked up another runner-up finish at Darlington in August. He also won a pair of ARCA events for Hendrick that year.

In 2004 he picked up five wins on the Busch series, and finished second in the drivers' standings behind Martin Truex, Jr., easily winning the rookie-of-the-year title. He also made his first Cup start early that season at, appropriately, Las Vegas, but finished a disappointing 41st, 39 spots lower than he would finish one year later.

Busch readily credits his older brother for a large part of his quick success in big-time racing, but it's clear that he's got a pretty deep reservoir of talent himself.

"Hopefully the sophomore slump won't be on the No. 5 car, and we can go out and try to earn some more respect out there," Busch said before the 2006 season.

He's already earned more respect than most people his age.

Busch celebrates after taking the Sony HD 500 in September 2005.

The DNFs aside, Busch made a tremendous full-season debut after getting a taste of Cup life with six starts for Hendrick Motorsports in 2004. His best finish that year was 24th, a high-water mark he erased by the third race in 2005, when he was runner-up at Las Vegas Motor Speedway.

DALE EARNHARDT JR.

It says a lot about star power that one of NASCAR's biggest worries in the fall of 2005 was that Dale Earnhardt Jr. did not qualify for the Chase.

Earnhardt Jr. is the world's favorite stock car racer, as evidenced by fans voting him the most popular driver for the third straight year in 2005, despite what was his worst season in Cup racing.

If 2004 was a memorable year for Earnhardt with a career-high six victories and his first win at the Daytona 500, the sequel was one he will try to forget. Struggling with cars that were generally below Dale Earnhardt Inc.'s standards, Earnhardt was rarely a factor in the Nextel Cup standings.

After finishing third at the Daytona, Earnhardt's 2005 was a mishmash of accidents, poor finishes and under-performances. He peaked a bit at mid-season with a victory at Chicagoland in the 18th race, but that was an illusion. By the time 26 races had passed, paring the Chase field to the elite 10, Earnhardt stood only 17th. He would drop to 19th by season's end, his worst finish in his six full years of Cup racing.

"I was worried that I was going to go winless this year," Earnhardt said with relief after the Chicago victory. And his worries were well-founded. He didn't win again, the first time since his five-race initiation into Cup racing in 1999 that he hadn't taken at least two victories.

NO. **8**

BORN: **October 10, 1974**

HOMETOWN: **Kannapolis, N.C.**

TEAM: **Dale Earnhardt Inc.**

CAR: **Chevrolet**

SPONSOR: **Budweiser**

CUP WINS: **16**

2005 CUP EARNINGS: **$5,761,632**

CAREER EARNINGS: **$35 million**

Although he has not been dominant, the red number 8 of Dale Earnhardt Jr. is still extremely popular on the Cup circuit.

"This is by no means the worst rut that anyone has ever been in, but it's pretty tough," Earnhardt said late in the frustrating season. "I've learned a lot about myself."

And he's learned a lot about how not to run a season.

Earnhardt Jr.'s problems probably originated in the off-season, after he had finished fifth in the 2004 Nextel Cup standings, with six wins and 16 top-five placings. DEI owner, Teresa Earnhardt, decided to swap pit crews between Earnhardt Jr. and stablemate Michael Waltrip. Earnhardt's crew chief and uncle, Tony Eury Sr., became DEI's director of motor sports, and Pete Rondeau succeeded him as crew chief. But continuous bad placings, including a 32nd and

a 42nd after the strong opening at the Daytona 500, got Rondeau reassigned during the season, and shop boss Steve Hmiel took over on an interim basis.

That was too much organizational change, and it showed on the track. For 2006, Tony Eury Jr. was back as crew chief, and the organization admitted they'd made a huge mistake in 2005.

It was a sudden and unanticipated reversal for a driver and shop on the ascendancy. In the Chase's first season, in 2004, Earnhardt led with nine races to go and seemed poised to win his first Nextel Cup. But he had back-to-back accidents at Martinsville and Atlanta. In the 10 races of the Chase, Earnhardt Jr.

won twice and was third twice but also had a 23rd and two 33rds. Those were enough to drop him to fifth in the consistency-oriented standings and foreshadowed some of the bottom-of-the-pack finishes of 2005.

But 2004? Now there was a season. It began with Earnhardt Jr. dominating Speedweek at Daytona, winning the Gatorade 125, the Busch race and his first 500, six years to the day after his famous father won the world's most famous stock car race for the first time. It came three years after Dale Sr. died there in the same race in which his protégé, Michael Waltrip, won and his son finished second.

"My dad was in the passenger seat, having a ball," Earnhardt said after his win at the 500. "Every time we come to Daytona we all feel it. In a way, it feels like you're closer to Dad. This is the greatest day of my life. I don't know if I'll ever be able to tell this story to anybody and really get it right."

He's always got Daytona right. Five months after his father was killed there, he won the Pepsi 400 on the famous Daytona track. DEI excels at restrictor track races, and Earnhardt has also won five times at Talladega.

There wasn't much doubt that Earnhardt Jr. would make the big time. His grandfather Ralph was NASCAR Sportsman Division champion in 1956, and Dale Sr. won a record-tying seven premier Cup series championships. Little E's first car was a 1978 Monte Carlo he and brother Kerry bought for $500. Dale, Kerry and their sister Kelly all raced against each other.

Earnhardt Jr. started racing in street stocks at the age of 17, and won three NASCAR Late Model feature races from 1994 to 1996. He was racing full-time on the Busch Series by 1998, when he won seven races, three poles and the drivers' championship. He won the title again in 1999 and made five appearances on the Winston Cup circuit.

With a massive five-year sponsorship from Budweiser, Earnhardt Jr. graduated to full-time Cup racing in 2000. He finished 16th in Cup points, losing rookie of the year to Matt Kenseth by 42 points and winning twice in his first

16 Cup appearances, matching Davey Allison's record, set in 1987.

He continued to gain victories and fans, finishing third in the Winston Cup standings in 2003, and eighth in 2004 before his disastrous 2005. And his legion of followers, many of them inherited from his late father, never deserted him.

"It's one thing to have fan support when you're riding high," Earnhardt Jr. said. "It's another thing to have it during the rough times."

And 2005 was the rough times.

Earnhardt Jr. gets his 17th Cup win at Richmond in May 2006. After lighting the tires up, he celebrates the Crown Royal 400 victory with the crew.

CARL EDWARDS

NO. 99

BORN: August 15, 1979

HOMETOWN: Columbia, Mo.

TEAM: Roush Racing

CAR: Ford

SPONSOR: Office Depot

CUP WINS: 4

2005 CUP EARNINGS: $4,889,993

CAREER EARNINGS: $6.2 million

A month into his first full Nextel Cup season, Carl Edwards' life changed, probably forever.

In mid-March 2005, he won both the Busch and Cup races at Atlanta Motor Speedway. No one in NASCAR history had ever accomplished his first wins in two different series on the same weekend, and instead of "Carl Who?" Carl Edwards became a household name.

He had gone door-to-door with Jimmie Johnson, beaten him on the final lap, and showed that he wasn't merely a nice, enthusiastic guy with a big smile, who did a backflip off his car's window ledge to celebrate a win. He is also a hungry, driven competitor.

After Atlanta the No. 99 team, which began

the year uncertain it had enough sponsorship money to complete it, no longer had to worry. And Edwards was headed toward a season for the ages.

By the time it was over, the once-unheralded son of a midwest racing legend was the talk of NASCAR Nation. He finished third in both the Nextel Cup and Busch Series, had a chance to win the Cup championship right into the final race of the year and took the Busch rookie-of-the-year award. He also would have won Cup rookie honors but had raced a few too many times the previous year.

"After that first win at Atlanta, everything kind of changed," Edwards understated. "It went from, 'Wow, we'd be super happy to run

in the top five' to 'Winning felt awfully good, we'd like to do it again every week.' "

He didn't win every week but he contended most weeks, and he picked up four victories, the most ever by a Cup driver in his first full season. Edwards had raced 13 times in 2004 as the mid-season replacement for Jeff Burton, who moved over to Richard Childress Racing, which may have made him ineligible for the 2005 rookie-of-the-year award but clearly helped him with his steep learning curve.

Like many new Cup drivers, he had been plagued by the "illusion that if I didn't win every race, that was failure," but 2004 and the early part of 2005 helped wean him off that win-at-all-costs mentality. He also had lots of help from the other four Roush drivers, all of whom qualified for the Chase.

Edwards, who dates model and Olympic swimmer Amanda Beard, became more patient on the track during the second half of 2005. In the Chase, which he entered in eighth place, he had the best average finish, at 8.4, and recorded seven top-10s. Two of those were his back-to-back victories at Atlanta, again, and Texas, when he rode the high groove to wins, a practice he'd got into during his formative years at the track in Holt Summit, Missouri.

In the end, Edwards couldn't quite catch Tony Stewart for the drivers' championship, tying teammate Greg Biffle for second,

"Carl Who" tests the new surface at Lowe's Motor Speedway in May 2006. The Missouri native took four wins in the Roush Racing Ford in 2005.

"They just kept giving me great cars with great engines."

35 points back. He was relegated to third because Biffle had two more victories.

"They just kept giving me great cars with great engines," Edwards said of his stupendous breakthrough season.

It was a far cry from just a few years earlier when he couldn't get any cars. He placed an ad in a racing trade paper, saying, partly, "Explore your options for next year. Have shoe, will travel."

Edwards was trying hard at a variety of racing gigs, but as recently as 2001, he was handing out business cards that read, "Will work for gas," teaching school part-time, living in his mother's basement and running USAC Silver Crown pavement races with little success.

It wasn't what Edwards had hoped for when he started racing four-cylinder mini-sprints in 1993 at the age of 13. His father, Carl Sr. ("Mike"), won more than 200 Modified stock cars and Midget races at midwestern tracks, and his son caught the bug. After his first year in Mini-Sprints, Edwards started winning regularly, picking up 18 victories over the next three seasons.

Then he moved into Modifieds and won the 1998 rookie-of-the-year title at Capital Speedway in Holt Summit. He won the NASCAR Dodge Weekly championship at Capital with 13 Modified feature wins in 1999, and took the

Pro Modifieds track championship in 2000.

After struggling in 2001, he won the 2002 Baby Grand Stock Car Association national championship and also made seven Craftsman Truck Series starts for Mittler Brothers Motorsports, finishing in the top 10 once. Jack Roush signed him to drive trucks for 2003, and he subsequently took rookie-of-the-year honors with three victories and 13 top fives.

When Edwards won the 2004 Daytona 500 truck race, Roush decided he'd found his replacement for Mark Martin, who was set to retire in three years. The plan was to ease Edwards through trucks and a couple of years on the Busch circuit and then have him take him over the No. 6 Nextel Cup car. But when Burton bolted for RCR in mid-season, Roush accelerated Edwards' career and sat him in Burton's car for the rest of the season.

And by March of 2005, he was the hottest thing in racing.

"I'm grateful to Jack for letting me do it," Edwards said. "The perspective has changed, the expectation has changed. Over all, this season has been one of just achieving, you know, dreams. We hoped for this, and now we kind of raised the bar for our ourselves."

And how.

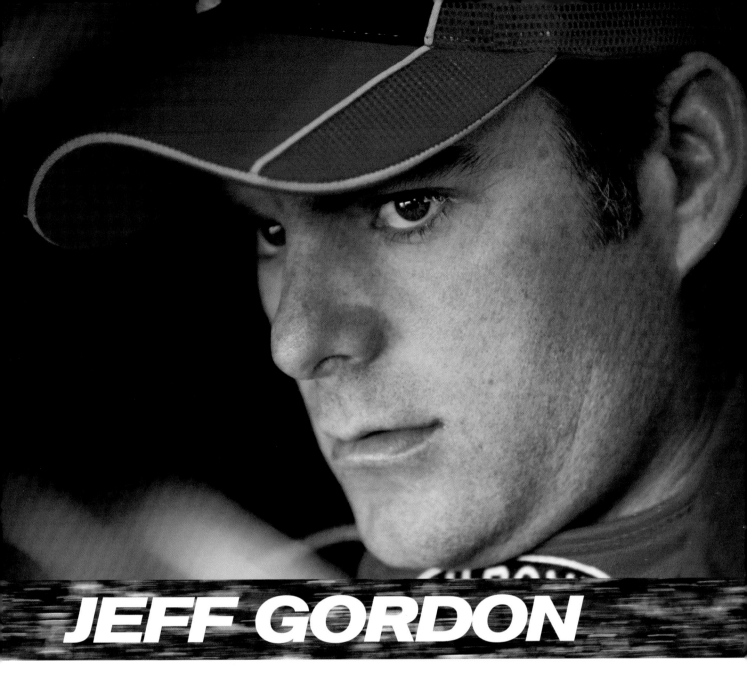

JEFF GORDON

In Jeff Gordon's mind, 2005 wasn't three-quarters empty, it was one-quarter full. It had to be. There was no other way to draw something positive from the superstar's worst finish since his rookie season.

After nearly winning the Nextel Cup title in 2004, finishing just 18 points behind winner Kurt Busch in third place, the four-team Cup champion didn't even qualify for the Chase in 2005. That unexpected failure led to his crew chief Robbie Loomis giving way to Steve Letarte for the final 10 races.

"Our focus in the final 10 was not points but to make our team better for next year," Gordon said. "And I think we did."

Enough that by Christmas the No. 24 Chevy was already the oddsmakers' early favorite to win the 2006 Daytona 500.

But then, Gordon won the season's most prestigious race in 2005, and had three victories by May 1, suggesting that he was on the way to his fifth Cup, just two behind record-holding icons Dale Earnhardt Sr. and Richard Petty. By mid-summer, that was clearly a pipe dream, as Gordon, his crew and his car struggled as much as they ever had in his brilliant 13-year career. There was a 16-race stretch leading into the Chase when he had only one top-five finish, and another horrific stint from mid-May to mid-July, when Gordon finished 30th or worse in six of eight races, to drop from second in

NO. 24

BORN:
August 4, 1971

HOMETOWN:
Vallejo, Calif.

TEAM: Hendrick Motorsports

CAR: Chevrolet

SPONSOR: DuPont, Pepsi, Nicorette

CUP WINS: 73

2005 CUP EARNINGS:
$6,855,444

CAREER EARNINGS:
$73.7 million

Jeff Gordon leads the pack in one of the races of the Gatorade Duel at Daytona in February 2006. The former USAC Midget star had problems in the follow-up Daytona 500, placing 25th.

the points standings to an unfamiliar 15th. After his Talladega triumph on May 1, he didn't win again until the second Martinsville race on October 23, to start an encouraging final month, when he had three top-three finishes in five races.

That was enough to move him up to 11th overall, and earn the $1 million bonus awarded to the driver who finishes Best of the Rest. Gordon, however, is not into consolation prizes and it's wise to remember that after finishing ninth in 2000 and being written off as a perennial contender, he rebounded to win the then-Winston Cup in 2000 and didn't finish below fourth until 2005.

It's evident that Gordon and his car still have the mustard, but they were missing consistency. Despite a stunning 12 races where he was 30th or lower, Gordon had four wins in 2005, just one fewer than in a 2004 season that was

highlighted by his fourth win at the Brickyard 400, catapulting him into historic company. Only he, A.J. Foyt, Rick Mears and Al Unser have won four times at Indianapolis Motor Speedway.

Indy is better known for open-wheel racing, which was Gordon's background and his biggest hurdle in gaining popularity with NASCAR fans. When he switched to stock car racing in late 1990, he was greeted with stiff resistance, even boos, because he was regarded as an outsider: a Californian who was too corporate, too well-spoken, too smooth and a little too successful. But this is what NASCAR management loved in their bid to gain mainstream approval and move to a more urban market. His poise, good looks and thirst for checkered flags eventually won over a large segment of the sport's fan base, although he and his Rainbow Warriors (the colorfully uniformed crew) still have plenty of detractors.

Gordon says, "All my life I've been pushed to do things at a young age that nobody else had done before," and history agrees with him.

His stepfather, John Bickford, bought him a Quarter Midget car when Gordon was only four. By the age of 6, he had won 35 main events. At 9, he won 46 of the 50 events he entered, and he won four national karting titles in his youth. He was so obviously heading toward a racing career that his parents moved from California to Pittsboro, Indiana. At age 16, he was the youngest person ever awarded a license to drive in the USAC and he had won over 100 races by the time he finished high school.

In 1990 Gordon won the USAC Midget championship at the age of 19, the youngest in history to do so. But later that year he attended Buck Baker's Driving School at North Carolina Speedway, fell in love with stock cars, told his stepfather that he was switching allegiance to NASCAR and teamed up with owner Bill Davis.

In 1991 he was Busch Series rookie of the year and a year later set a Busch Series record with 11 poles, three of those resulting in wins. Rick Hendrick watched him win a race at Atlanta in March 1992 despite his car falling apart around him, and signed him for the Winston Cup. He made his debut in the final 1992 race at Atlanta, and finished 31st.

Gordon was the Winston Cup rookie of the year in 1993, becoming the first rookie in 30 years to win a qualifying race for the Daytona 500. He got his first win in 1994, at the Coca-Cola 600 and won the inaugural Brickyard 400, which he says, "elevated me to a new level." He finished eighth in points, but was struggling with consistency, just as he would 11 years later, and had 10 DNFs.

But in 1995, Gordon shed that inconsistency with only three DNFs, and had seven wins and 23 top-10s to become the youngest Cup-winning champion of the modern era. That initiated one of the greatest four-year stretches in NASCAR history, as Gordon won three titles and finished runner-up in the other,

losing by only 37 points to teammate Terry Labonte. He won 40 races over those four years.

On the way to his second Cup series title in 1997, he became the youngest driver (26) to win the Daytona 500. In capturing his third title in 1998, he tied Richard Petty's modern-era record of 13 wins, tied the Cup record of four straight wins and collected a then-record $9.3 million.

After a couple of slumping years (seventh, ninth), Gordon won the title again in 2001, before finishing fourth, fourth and third heading into his confusing 2005 season.

For most drivers, 11th place and a $1 million bonus would be a decent season, but Gordon is not most drivers.

"I'm not that interested in finishing 11th," he said during the Chase.

He never has been.

Gordon's star has dimmed a bit, but the three-time Daytona 500 winner is still a major player in Cup racing.

Gordon told his stepfather, "Sell everything. We're going stock car racing."

KEVIN HARVICK

NO. 29

BORN: December 8, 1975

HOMETOWN: Bakersfield, Calif.

TEAM: Richard Childress Racing

CAR: Chevrolet

SPONSOR: Goodwrench, Reese's

CUP WINS: 5

2005 CUP EARNINGS: $4,970,049

CAREER EARNINGS: $24.6 million

Kevin Harvick's nickname is "Happy," but maybe he should change it to "Interesting" or "Vocal."

Life is never dull around the Richard Childress Racing No. 29 car. Harvick can be winning races one week, igniting controversy the next. But whatever week it is, Harvick will call it as he sees it at the time.

"To me, you should always speak your mind," the fiery California-born driver explains. "With me, you're going to get an honest answer, and you're not going to get a bunch of bull in the middle of it."

Harvick, then, was straight-up about 2005, a year which started hot and ended as cool as the previous one, with the same result: 14th place in the drivers' standings and an outsider's look at the Chase for the Nextel Cup.

"It wasn't the season we expected," Harvick conceded after he had only three top-five finishes, all in the first 11 weeks of the 2005 calendar. "But it wasn't a complete wash either."

Harvick did rebound from a winless 2004 season to take the checkered flag at Bristol in the season's fifth race, raising hopes that he might break through into the superstardom expected of one of only five men to have won races in all three of NASCAR's national series.

But despite strong performances on NASCAR's short tracks, for much of the season Harvick had trouble with his Chevy and sometimes with other drivers. The car troubles were

serious enough that Childress made changes in his company's engine department.

Harvick had a serious confrontation with Joe Nemechek after a crash in February, and again in May. Greg Biffle called him "a punk" after a Busch race at Chicagoland, which harkened back to their confrontation after a Busch race three years earlier. And his crew chief, Todd Berrier, was suspended for four races for using an illegal fuel cell in the qualifier at Las Vegas in March. Berrier incurred another suspension in October.

Although Harvick rallied nicely to win the Bristol two weeks after the fuel-cell suspension, there followed a wildly inconsistent stretch when he was 22nd or lower six times in 16 races. And by June there was speculation that Harvick might be moving to Penske. He committed to a return to Childress when the owner promised improvements to the entire organization.

But the worst part of Harvick's 2005 had nothing to do with his passionate personality, with his busy schedule or with RCR. In November, his wife DeLana's father died. Later that week, he won his fourth Busch race of the season at Texas, with a lightning-quick pit late in the race.

"It's been a tough week, I want to thank all (his crew), my wife, everybody," he said, fighting back tears. "It's been the hardest week I've ever had to go through."

Kevin Harvick (29) leads Dale Jarrett in the Dodge Charger 500 in May 2006. The Childress Racing driver, who has five Cup wins to his credit, took 14th at this Darlington Raceway event.

Harvick and Joe Nemechek about to have some words after an on-track altercation.

Harvick says that with RCR's improvement, his results will get better, too. His back-to-back 14th-place finishes were major detours on what appeared to be a direct road to the top after he won the rookie-of-the-year award in 2001. He did so despite bearing the weight of taking over the Chevrolet when Dale Earnhardt was killed at Daytona. Although Childress changed the number from 3 to 29 and the base color from black to white, Harvick was known as the man who replaced Earnhardt.

It was an incredibly successful and varied debut Cup season, as Harvick won in his third-ever start (Atlanta) nipping Jeff Gordon by .006 of a second, captured the inaugural race at Chicagoland, had 16 top-10s, and finished ninth overall. He also won the Busch series and with one ride in Craftsman Trucks, competed in 69 races at 30 different tracks in NASCAR's top three divisions, covering 20,000 racing miles. This was a very busy man.

Harvick endured NASCAR's typical sophomore slump in 2002, dropping to 21st in points, but did win at Chicagoland again. There were six DNFs, the most in his career, but also a Craftsman Truck victory, which gave him a win in each of NASCAR's big three series. And there was the run-in with Biffle and a suspension for spinning another driver in a truck race.

When Berrier took over as crew chief for 2003, and Harvick responded with a victory at Indianapolis and a fifth-place finish in the points, he was back on the career path that began in kindergarten when his parents bought him a go-kart. Over the next decade, he won seven national titles and two Grand National championships. At 18, he won the Late Model title at Mesa Marin raceway in his hometown of Bakersfield. Two years later he was rookie of the year in NASCAR's Elite Division Featherlite Southwest Series, finishing 11th in points.

In 1998 he won the NASCAR Grand National Winston West Series championship, and the next year he drove Craftsman Trucks, with 11 top-10 finishes. Childress, impressed with Harvick's hard-driving style, gave him a ride in the Busch Series, and he won three times in 2000, was rookie of the year and finished third in points. The plan was to go full-bore for the Busch driver's title in 2001, until he was suddenly promoted to replace the late Earnhardt. He became the first driver ever to win a Busch title and the Cup rookie of the year in the same season.

Through it all, he has been self-confident, often testy and usually brutally honest. After the 2005 season, he told NASCAR.com, "We have fallen a bit short of our expectations. I am chomping at the bit to redeem ourselves."

DALE JARRETT

Dale Jarrett grew up in the home of a racing legend, and has become one himself, so he knows the code.

"We get paid to race, and to race hard, no matter what the circumstances," Jarrett said about his dissatisfying 2005 season.

The circumstances for 2005 included missing the Chase, a second successive 15th-place finish in the points standing, leading very few laps all season, changing crew chiefs twice, and struggling with downforce on the intermediate tracks.

But when you race hard, you can discover a diamond among all the coal, and Jarrett found it in early October at Talladega. No. 88 managed to navigate himself through a

demolition derby that featured two eight-car crashes, for Ford's first victory at Talladega in two years, and Jarrett's first victory anywhere in 98 races.

"At this stage, you're not exactly sure when that last victory is going to be there, so you learn to cherish each one," said the 1999 Cup champion, who was just a few weeks shy of his 49th birthday when he took Talladega.

Until that October race, Jarrett led only two laps all season, and, in response, owner Robert Yates shifted Billy Wilburn to crew chief in late spring, replacing Mike Ford, and then brought in veteran Todd Parrott in September. By season's end, he had hired Slugger Labbe to crew chief Jarrett for 2006.

NO. 88

BORN: November 26, 1956

HOMETOWN: Hickory, N.C.

TEAM: Robert Yates Racing

CAR: Ford

SPONSOR: UPS

CUP WINS: 32

2005 CUP EARNINGS: $4,705,436

CAREER EARNINGS: $51.6 million

Jarrett did spend eight weeks in a top-10 position and stood ninth with just five races to go before the Chase, but consecutive results of 34th, 31st, 24th, and 39th pushed him out of the hunt.

"You can't be pleased with the season," said Jarrett, who wasn't too pleased with the previous two either.

In 2003 Jarrett fell out of the top 10 for the first time in seven years, with a 26th-place finish, although he did win at Rockingham in February.

In 2004 Jarrett doubled his top-10 finishes from the previous year, from seven to 14, but the unthinkable happened. For the first time since 1992, he did not win a Cup race. That ended his pursuit of Richard Petty's all-time record of 18 straight seasons with at least one win.

Winning and the surname Jarrett had long ago become synonymous in NASCAR circles. Dale's father, Ned, won 50 Cup races, and took the series championship in 1961 and 1965.

But when he was young, Jarrett's sporting future seemed headed for a different kind of course. He was offered a full golf scholarship at the University of North Carolina, and his father thought he'd become a pro in that sport. Jarrett was also a star high-school football, baseball and basketball player. It wasn't until he was 20 that he and a couple of friends put together a car for Jarrett to enter in the Limited Sportsman Division at Hickory Motor Speedway, the hometown track where he'd done odd jobs.

In 1982 he became a charter member of NASCAR's Busch Series, competing in its first official season. When he moved up to fourth in the Busch points standings in 1984, he started landing Winston Cup rides and raced for eight different owners over the next four years. He had only two top-five finishes in 67 Cup races over that span, but he was faring well in Busch and eventually won 11 races and 14 poles before leaving the series in 1999.

In 1989, Jarrett recorded five top-10 Winston Cup finishes for Cale Yarborough, and the next year, the Wood Brothers hired him to replace Neil Bonnett. In 1991, at Michigan his first career Cup win also gave the Woods their first victory in 134 races.

When Joe Gibbs, the famous football coach, started a NASCAR team in 1992, he contracted Jarrett as his first driver. After a 19th place finish in their first season together, Jarrett won the 1993 Daytona 500 to give the Gibbs team its inaugural Cup victory. Gibbs still refers to it as the biggest thrill of his ownership career, and it launched Jarrett's win-per-season streak that lasted until 2003.

After one more year with Gibbs, Jarrett joined Robert Yates Racing in 1995 in the No. 28 car, replacing the badly injured Ernie Irvan. He won at Pocono, but a 13th-place points finish didn't indicate what Yates and Jarrett were about to begin.

They opened the 1996 season with a win at Daytona, won again at Charlotte, Indianapolis and Michigan, and Jarrett leapt all the way up to third in the points standings.

He won seven races in 1997, the most of his career, and lost the points title by just 14 points to Jeff Gordon. Two years later, he opened the season winning the Daytona 500 again and closed it with the points championship, finishing comfortably ahead of Bobby Labonte. The run to the title included four victories, a stunning 24 top-five finishes and Driver of the Year honors from virtually every poll. That made the Jarretts only the second father/son team (after Lee and Richard Petty) to take stock car racing's top points prize.

"I'm a believer that things are brought to you when you're ready for them," said the late-bloomer. "It's just taken me a long time to be ready for this."

Jarrett extended his streak to six years in the upper five of the points standings by finishing fourth, with two victories, in 2000, and fifth, with four wins, in 2001. He won twice in 2002, but slipped to ninth with eight DNFs, his highest total in 11 years.

That was the last year he finished in the top 10, but he believes, as long as he keeps racing hard, he will eventually be racing for the Nextel Cup championship.

"At this stage, you're not exactly sure when that last victory is going to be there, so you learn to cherish each one."

Opposite: Veteran Dale Jarrett (88) with Jeff Gordon at Talladega. The driver of the UPS car, Jarrett has won over 30 Cup races and over $50 million since 1984.

JIMMIE JOHNSON

NO. 48

BORN: September 17, 1975

HOMETOWN: El Cajon, Calif.

TEAM: Hendrick Motorsports

CAR: Chevrolet

SPONSOR: Lowe's

CUP WINS: 18

2005 CUP EARNINGS: $6,796,664

CAREER EARNINGS: $26.6 million

Soon – very soon, according to most NASCAR reviews – Jimmie Johnson's No. 48 car will live up to his crew chief's description.

"This is a championship caliber team and it has been since its inception, thanks to Rick Hendrick and Jeff Gordon," Chad Knaus told Nascar.com.

In his first four full years on the Nextel Cup circuit Johnson, driving a Chevrolet owned by Gordon as part of Hendrick Motorsports' stable, has finished second in the points race twice and fifth twice.

The communication between Knaus and Johnson is often called the best driver-chief relationship in the business and combined with the solid Hendrick cars, has led to 18 wins in the team's inaugural four years.

In 2005 Johnson led the points race for a total of 16 weeks, but crashed at the Brickyard 400 in the first week of August, finishing 38th, had his engine conk out at Bristol late in the month, finishing 36th, and then two weeks later was 25th at Richmond.

With four race wins, Johnson finished fifth overall in 2005. That was a terrific result, but much lower than anticipated after he opened with seven straight top-10s, including a victory (Las Vegas), two seconds and a third in the season's first seven races.

In 2004 Johnson had been even better, losing the title to Kurt Busch by only eight points,

the tightest margin in Cup history. He led the series with a remarkable eight wins and 20 top-five finishes, and would have won the points race had Busch not made a phenomenal recovery in the final race. Again, late summer was the only thing standing between Johnson and the drivers' championship as he scuffled through four races in August, which whittled away at his lead of 200-plus points. But his finish of four victories and a second in the season's final six races was the stuff of legend and foreshadowed his quick start in 2005.

Johnson, Knaus and everyone else at Hendrick Motorsports were hoping for a drivers' title to take at least a bit of the terrible sting out of the 2004 season, when an October plane crash near Martinsville claimed the lives of 10 people associated with the organization, including Rick Hendrick's son Ricky and brother John. Johnson had won the Martinsville race that day and, under unfathomable emotional weight, also won the next week at Atlanta as part of his three consecutive victories late in the Chase.

After rebounding from that kind of life tragedy, it's no wonder that it seemed like nothing for Johnson's team to be able to recover from a 40th place at the 2005 Chevy 400 to winning the next race, the Coca-Cola 600. In other back-to-back rallies, Johnson finished 36th one week, sixth the next; 31st, then sixth; 38th, then fifth.

"We can bounce back from anything, easy,"

Jimmie Johnson spinning during the Nextel All-Star Challenge in May 2004 – definitely not a common sight.

A strong performer, Johnson has been to Victory Lane many times, and his Lowe's-sponsored Chevy is a familiar sight in the winner's circle (above). Johnson, shown at Talladega (opposite), won almost $6.8 million in 2005.

The California native began racing motocross at the age of four and gravitated toward open-wheel racing.

says Knaus. And that's because the car, crew and driver are strong and consistent. Johnson's magnificent streak of 70 straight weeks in NASCAR's top 10 – the ninth longest of all time – was halted, if only briefly, in the second week of 2004.

While Johnson showed promise in his early years as a driver, he is one of the rare professional athletes who has made a bigger impact in the major leagues than he did in the minors.

The California native began racing motocross at the age of four and gravitated toward open-wheel racing. When he entered the fledgling Mickey Thompson Stadium Truck Series at the age of 15, he was the youngest driver ever to compete in the series. The next year, he won the first of his three Thompson series titles, and also took three other major off-road crowns: the 1994 SCORE desert racing championship and the 1996 and 1997 SODA Winter Series championships.

In 1998 Johnson took up the challenge of stock car racing and was rookie of the year in the ASA Challenge series. He continued with ASA, but also got five NASCAR Busch series rides in 1999.

Driving for Herzog Motorsports, he was eighth in the Busch Series in 2001, and Hendrick tried him in three Winston Cup races. His best finish was 25th at Homestead,

so it was startling when he won the pole in the Daytona 500 the following February. He was just the third rookie in the modern era to start the Daytona 500 on the pole and did it in fewer starts than any of them. Nine starts later, he had his first Cup win at, appropriately, California.

Johnson won three times in his rookie season, and a third-place finish at Atlanta in March vaulted him into the top 10 of the points standing for the first time. He didn't drop out of that exalted company until February, two years later.

Without doubt the presence of Gordon as a teammate, mentor and friend has been invaluable to Johnson's quick rise into the upper echelons of stock car racing. He has often been called a Gordon clone for his good looks and charm, although there was some unanticipated controversy in 2005. His crew exploited a rules loophole, which was closed immediately after their win at Dover, to improve shock performances. And the next week Johnson was criticized for his role in a crash at Talladega.

"It was sad, disappointing to not win the championship," Johnson said after the 2005 season. "To win is what we're here for, and coming so close (in 2004), in our minds there's really nowhere else to go but to win the championship."

KASEY KAHNE

NO. **9**

BORN: **April 10, 1980**

HOMETOWN: **Enumclaw, Wash.**

TEAM: **Evernham Motorsports**

CAR: **Dodge**

SPONSOR: **Dodge Dealers**

CUP WINS: **1**

2005 CUP EARNINGS: **$4,874,838**

CAREER EARNINGS: **$10.2 million**

The Sophomore Slump is a common pit stop for a NASCAR driver.

But if you have to go through the second-year blues, it's nice to hear the sweet music of your first Nextel Cup victory.

Kasey Kahne, a core member of NASCAR's Young Guns, backslid in the 2005 season, struggling with his car most of the year. After winning rookie of the year in 2004 with 13 top-fives and a 13th-place finish in the points standing, the popular driver from the U.S. Northwest plunged to 23rd in 2005.

However, there was that unforgettable Saturday night in May when Kahne outdueled Tony Stewart, one of his idols, to win the Chevy 400 at Richmond. Kahne's pit crew got him back

on the track more quickly than Stewart's did off the final pit, and he held off the eventual 2005 points champion. In his 47th start, after six runner-up finishes, Kahne finally had his first Nextel Cup checkered flag.

"It's easily the best night I've ever had in a race car," Kahne told *Sports Illustrated*. "We'd come so close to winning, so many times. To get to Victory Lane was a huge relief. The best thing about it is that I don't have to answer, 'When are you finally going to win?' anymore."

After the race Stewart leaned into the window of the No. 9 car and told Kahne that "nobody could take this from me and that it was an honor to finish second in my first win."

The victory, the first by a Dodge Charger

since Neil Bonnett in 1977, came in the 11th race of the season and prompted predictions that Kahne was ready to resume pursuit of a berth in the Chase. It was his fourth top-five in the first 11 races and came after he'd won his second consecutive pole.

Kahne's season spiked on that night, however, and he enjoyed only four top-10 finishes in the remaining 25 races.

"We had a lot of potential this year, but couldn't seem to get the chemistry or communication of the team just right, and I seemed to fight the race car all year long," Kahne said.

By the start of 2006, Kahne had lost crew chief Tommy Baldwin Jr. and team owner Ray Evernham had made radical organizational changes, installing Kenny Francis as "Team Director" for the No. 9 car. Kahne hoped the reorganization would help him get back on his mercurial career path.

Kahne grew up on a track, an eighth-of-a-mile oval with banked turns that his father Kelly built for him on the family's 50-acre plot in Enumclaw, Washington. When he was 8 years old, he began racing four-wheelers against his friends on that track before graduating to the dirt ovals around Washington State. He moved up quickly, winning 11 of the 14 races, the Hannigan Speedway championship and the Northwest Mini-Sprint Car title when he was 16. At 18, he won a dozen full-sized Sprint car races.

Now 26, Kasey Kahne came into NASCAR with 13 top fives in 2004. Here he's shown in the Evernham Dodge in the Pennsylvania 500 at Pocono in 2005.

Kahne, seen here during a pit stop at Darlington, ran in several open-wheel series including USAC and the Toyota Atlantic Series before getting into a Busch car in 2002.

"We'd come so close to winning, so many times. To get to Victory Lane was a huge relief."

Legendary car owner Steve Lewis signed Kahne to run a full USAC schedule of Sprint, Midget and Silver Crown Series cars in 2000, and he also raced limited schedules in the Toyota Atlantic Series and the Formula Ford 2000 Series. In 2000 he won the Midget championship and was rookie of the year in the Silver Bullet series.

In 2002 he jumped from open wheel to NASCAR's Busch Series, driving for Robert Yates in 2002 and Akins Motorsports in 2003. He finished seventh in 2003, and won his first Busch race in the final event of the season at Homestead.

"It took almost two years but it actually felt that much better when we finally did win a race," Kahne said, not suspecting he would undergo a similar experience in Nextel Cup. Evernham signed him to start the 2004 season in the No. 9 Dodge, replacing icon Bill Elliott, who was moving into semi-retirement.

His first Nextel start was an unimpressive 41st at the 2004 Daytona 500, but in the next three races he had two seconds and a third, making him just the seventh driver in Cup history to record three top-fives in the first four starts of his career. He eventually had five second-place finishes on the way to rookie-of-the-year honors, and nearly qualified for the Chase, standing ninth just one race before the cutoff. But a 24th at the Chevy 400 dropped him to 12th and out of contention. Still, it was a tremendous rookie season, which he finished off with three fifth-place finishes in the final four races.

Then came the dreaded Sophomore Slump in 2005.

"I've made plenty of mistakes," he said after the season. "I've learned a lot, but I've still got a long way to go."

MATT KENSETH

It's become clear in recent Cup seasons that winning the most doesn't always mean winning the biggest.

Matt Kenseth knows that drill off by heart. The pride of Cambridge, Wisconsin, won a series-high five races in 2002 and finished eighth in the Cup standings. The next year, he took just one checkered flag but captured the final drivers' championship of the Winston Cup era with a stunningly consistent season that would provide a template for future winners: Pile up those top-fives and top-10s; win enough races to keep the fires of hope burning; and avoid Did-Not-Finishes like the plague. It's a simple formula but very difficult to execute over a nine-month season.

Kenseth, one of the most even-keeled personalities on NASCAR's top circuit, has maintained a steady approach to Nextel Cup driving, and it helped him to back-to-back berths in the first two years of the Chase. Even in 2005, when he appeared hopelessly up the track in the points standings through the first 17 races, Kenseth's stable attitude and diligent Roush Racing crew kept the No. 17 Ford pointed in the right direction.

Finishes of eighth and seventh in 2004 and 2005 might pale beside the wild excitement of the 2003 championship season, but they emphasize Kenseth's mature consistency. Over a four-year period, he never finished below eighth in the points standings and totaled

NO. 17
BORN:
March 10, 1972
HOMETOWN:
Cambridge, Wis.
TEAM: Roush Racing
CAR: Ford
SPONSOR:
DeWalt Tools
CUP WINS: 10
2005 CUP EARNINGS:
$5,790,774
CAREER EARNINGS:
$32.1 million

Matt Kenseth, in his No. 17 DeWalt Ford, takes the green flag at the 2005 Dickies 500 at Texas Motor Speedway.

Opposite: Kenseth and the DeWalt Ford in pit lane after smacking the wall at the DirecTV 500, Martinsville, April 2006.

77 top-10 finishes. And 2005, in particular, emphasized that a driver should never lose sight of the finish line, no matter how far away it looks.

The first half of the 2005 season was crammed with bad omens. Kenseth blew an engine early in the Daytona 500 to open the year in 42nd place, the first time in 71 races that he was not in the Cup's top 10. Over the first dozen races of the schedule, he had just one top-10 finish. By the first week of June, he stood a whopping 700 points out of first place. Heading into the 18th race at Chicagoland, the season's mid-point, he had only one top-five result, standing 19th in the standings, and critics were strongly questioning his credentials as a Chase candidate. Kenseth later admitted he thought the same thing.

Then he finished second at Chicagoland.

"I think we can race our way into the Chase,"

Kenseth said, although few believed him at the time.

But after mid-summer, Kenseth was a threat to challenge on almost every weekend, and in the final 18 races of the season he had nine top-10s. When he won at Bristol in late August, breaking a victory drought that had reached 56 starts, he moved into 11th place, just a dozen points out of the all-important top 10.

Two races later, a runner-up finish at Richmond, the final event before the Chase, put him into eighth place as one of five Roush cars to qualify for the Chase.

He managed six top-fives in the Chase, but there were also three finishes below 25th, fatal blows to anyone with title hopes, and he ended the season in seventh. Still, Kenseth's 2005 season showed the value of persistence combining with talent.

Kenseth nurtured that talent as a mechanic

on the family car. His father Roy made a deal with his 13-year-old son that he would buy and race a stock car if Matt would work on it. Then, when he turned 16, Matt could drive the car on the demanding Wisconsin circuits.

That early crew training developed Kenseth's sensitive touch behind the wheel and he began to rise through the difficult ranks of the Midwest short tracks.

At 19, he became the youngest feature winner in the history of the ARTGO Challenge Series, breaking the record set by his Roush teammate Mark Martin. At 23, he won track titles at both Madison International Speedway and Wisconsin International Raceway. At 24, he finished third in the demanding Hooters Series. At 25, in 1997, he was in second place in the American Speed Association when Robbie Reiser invited him to race in NASCAR's Busch Grand National Series. In only 21 starts, he finished second in the rookie standings.

In 1998 Kenseth had three Busch wins and finished second to future rival Dale Earnhardt Jr. in the points standings. And he got into his first Cup race, finishing a remarkable sixth at Dover, subbing for legendary Bill Elliott.

Kenseth made five Cup starts for Roush Racing in 1999, and made the jump to a full schedule in 2000. He became the first rookie to win the Coca-Cola 600, had 11 top-10 finishes and was rookie of the year. The standard sophomore jinx hit him in 2001, when he didn't win a race, but he rebounded with a series-high five Winston Cup wins in 2002.

Then, in 2003, he grabbed the points lead on the fourth weekend and drove consistently and steadily to the last title of the Winston Cup era, despite winning just one race all year. He joined the late Alan Kulwicki as the only Wisconsin-bred Cup champions.

He followed that by winning the second and third races of 2004, finishing eighth overall and unleashing his mad dash into the 2005 Chase.

"I feel really good about our program," Kenseth says. "We have a lot to build on."

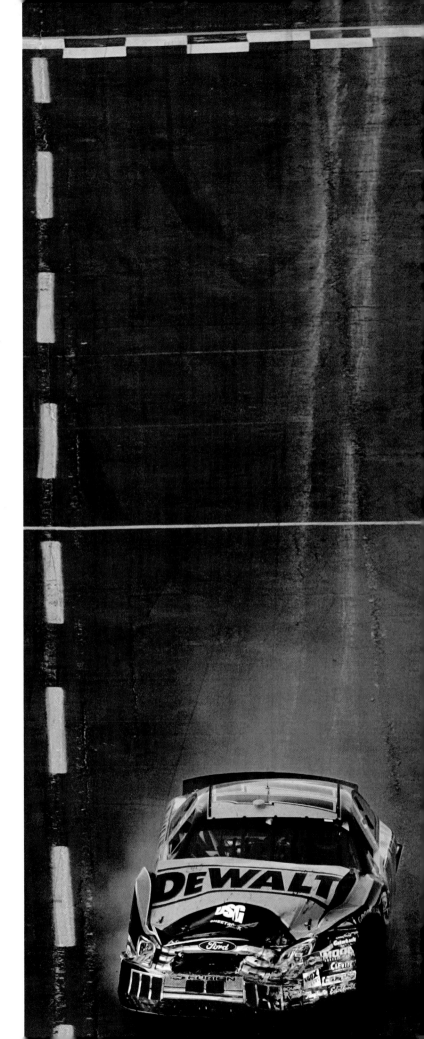

BOBBY LABONTE

NO. **43**

BORN: **May 8, 1964**

HOMETOWN:
Corpus Christi, Tex.

TEAM: **Petty Enterprises**

CAR: **Dodge**

SPONSOR: **Cheerios**

CUP WINS: **21**

2005 CUP EARNINGS:
$4,627,404

CAREER EARNINGS:
$45.4 million

He's got the Number, and he works for the Name.

After 11 years and a Winston Cup title with Joe Gibbs Racing, Bobby Labonte switched allegiances in 2006. He couldn't have stepped into larger shoes.

Labonte's car now sports the number 43, made famous by seven-time Cup champion Richard Petty. The racing legend is one of his bosses at Petty Enterprises, as is Kyle Petty, one of Labonte's best friends.

"We only live a half-a-mile from each other and our passion for racing and a lot of other things is the same," Labonte said of Kyle.

It was time for a change from Gibbs, where Labonte had hung his helmet since 1995. He

won 21 Cup races. But his final two years there weren't successful, by any measure.

In 2004, for the first time in nine years, he didn't win a race and finished 12th in the points standings, just the second season he hadn't been in the top 10 since he joined JGR.

In 2005 he plummeted all the way to 24th in the standings.

Always one to complete what he started – "I think I only failed to finish nine laps in 2000 when we won the championship," he recalls – Labonte suffered an uncharacteristic 10 DNFs in 2005, more than in the two previous years put together. He was essentially eliminated from the Chase over the final 10 races by his results in the first 10: just one top-10 finish,

and five DNFs. Hardly Labonte numbers.

"When you struggle, you question yourself and then you start trying harder or trying different things, and chances are you tried too hard," Labonte said of his frustrating final two seasons at Joe Gibbs Racing.

So, struggling, he turned to an organization that had also struggled, failing to produce a Cup race winner since John Andretti in 1999. But it's still the biggest name in the game. Petty Enterprises has been on the scene since NASCAR began, and was founded by legend Lee Petty and taken over by his even more successful son, the "King."

Labonte, of course, is quite accustomed to family connections. He and his older brother Terry are the only siblings to capture the drivers' points title on NASCAR's elite circuit. Terry was Winston Cup champion in 1984 and 1996, and Bobby won it in 2000.

The Labontes grew up in Corpus Christi, Texas, where Bobby started racing Quarter Midgets when he was 5 years old. He got into go-karts at 14, but the family then moved to North Carolina to further Terry's promising racing career.

As Terry drove for Hagan Racing, Bobby Labonte did the menial chores around the shop, and eventually graduated to pit crew. When Terry left to drive for Junior Johnson after the 1986 season, Bobby went to work for car builder Jay Hedgecock. He also raced Late

A veteran of Cup racing, Bobby Labonte is running with the most famous number in stock car racing on his Cheerios-sponsored Dodge.

Labonte in practice for the Dodge Charger 500 at Darlington. He started 11th in the May 2006 race, and finished 22nd.

"When you struggle, you question yourself and chances are you tried too hard."

Model stocks at Caraway Speedway in Asheboro and captured the 1987 track title.

After moving up to the Sportsmen's Series at Concord, Labonte graduated to a full NASCAR Busch Series schedule in 1990 and finished fourth in the points standings. The next year, he won the Busch championship and also entered his own car in a couple of Winston Cup races. In 1992 Labonte lost the Busch points title to Joe Nemechek by three points, still the closest finish in the history of NASCAR's three national series.

His Busch record landed Labonte a full-time Winston Cup ride with Bill Davis Racing in 1993. He finished 19th in his rookie year and slipped to 21st in 1994 before leaving to replace venerable Dale Jarrett in Joe Gibbs' No. 18. The move paid off right away, with his first career victory, at the Coca-Cola 600 in Charlotte, two wins at Michigan and 10th place in the final standings.

In 1996 Labonte won the final race of the year at Atlanta as his brother clinched his second Winston Cup title. Over the next two years he won three times, had 36 top top-10 finishes and climbed to sixth in the points standings.

Five wins and 23 top-5 results helped Labonte finish second in the 1999 points race, behind Jarrett.

Then, in the perfect season of 2000, he beat Dale Earnhardt for the championship, while winning four times and enduring only two finishes outside of the top 20. Of 10,167 laps that year, he failed to complete only nine.

After a sixth-place finish and two wins in 2001, Labonte slipped to 16th in 2002, prompting the team to switch crew chiefs and move from Pontiac to Chevrolet Monte Carlos for 2003. He climbed back to seventh in 2003, and won the final race of the Winston Cup era.

But in 2004, his nine-year streak of winning at least one race was broken; he had a terrible second half, and slipped to 12th. When that was followed by another struggling season, he joined the Pettys.

"I felt in my heart, 'Well if I had to drive for somebody else, who would it be for?'" he said. "It might not have been something that would have happened five or 10 years ago.

"But this is a great opportunity for me to drive for a great family and get the No. 43 back into Victory Lane."

STERLING MARLIN

When he was 15 years old, Sterling Marlin was changing tires on stock car No. 14. And now he's driving No. 14.

After the two-time Daytona 500 winner left Chip Ganassi Racing after the 2005 season to get a new start with MB2 Motorsports, he also changed numerals from 40 to 14, the same number his well-known father had driven.

Clifton "Coo Coo" Marlin was one of the sport's pioneers and is generally regarded as the first driver from central Tennessee to make a name for himself in NASCAR's elite series. He died in August 2005 and when his son switched teams, he also switched numbers in memory of his father.

"I started working on my dad's cars when I was 12 or so, then moved up to changing tires," Marlin recalls. "When I was 16, I acted as his crew chief, and started driving too."

Coo Coo Marlin never won a Winston Cup race, but the tough-minded racer made 165 starts in the premier series, with 51 top-10 finishes. He was a legend on the short tracks of Tennessee and Alabama, and established the record of four track championships at Tennessee Fairgrounds.

Sterling Marlin followed in those prominent footsteps and won three straight Tennessee Fairgrounds driving titles from 1980 to 1982.

By then, he'd also made a dozen NASCAR Cup starts, with his first one coming as a replacement for his father, who had injured his

NO. 14

BORN: June 30, 1956

HOMETOWN: Columbia, Tenn.

TEAM: MB2 Motorsports

CAR: Chevrolet

SPONSOR: Waste Management

CUP WINS: 10

2005 CUP EARNINGS: $4,080,118

CAREER EARNINGS: $36 million

Born in 1956, Sterling Marlin drives his MB Motorsports Chevy with No. 14 on its flanks, the same number that his father, "Coo Coo," drove with.

shoulder. Just 18, Marlin finished 29th in that debut at Nashville.

Riding the momentum of his three championships at Tennessee, Marlin signed with owner Roger Hamby for his first full NASCAR season in 1983, and won the rookie-of-the-year honors, finishing 19th overall.

But over the next three years, Marlin had only sporadic Cup starts, racing a total of just 32 times for six different owners.

When he accepted a full-time ride from Billy Hagan in 1987, Marlin showed what he could do, finishing 11th in the standings and recording four top-five finishes. He spent another three seasons with Hagan, nibbling around the top 10 in the standings, but never quite cracking it.

When Marlin moved over to Junior Johnson in 1991, he also moved up to seventh in the points race and was 10th the following season.

Then he jumped to the Stavola Brothers, finishing 15th in 1993.

By then, he had lined up for 278 Cup races, but still hadn't nailed down a victory. In spite of the win drought, Morgan-McClure signed Marlin for 1994 and he made an incredible debut, winning the Daytona 500.

"My fondest memory," Marlin says.

His father was watching the race and recalled, "When he won, it was a great, great moment."

The rest of the 1994 season couldn't come close to matching the opening race, as seven DNFs forced Marlin down into 14th place. But in 1995, he won the Daytona 500 again, matching legends Richard Petty and Cale Yarborough as the only drivers to win stock car racing's most prestigious event in back-to-back years. He also picked up victories at Darlington and Talladega, and leapt all the way to third in the points standings.

He finished eighth in 1996 with victories at the Talladega and the second Daytona event, but after he was winless in 1997 and dropped to 25th in the drivers' standings, Marlin moved over to Chip Ganassi's SABCO, where he would spend the next eight seasons.

After three years without a victory for Ganassi, in 2001 Marlin returned to the form of his best Morgan-McClure seasons, finishing third in the points race and hitting Victory Lane at Michigan and Charlotte. The win at Michigan was Dodge's first checkered flag in its return to Cup competition after being absent for two decades.

He won twice more in 2002 and might have won his third Daytona 500, but under a red flag, with Marlin in the lead, he was penalized for repairing some body damage and eventually finished eighth.

Marlin moved into the lead in the drivers' standings the next week, held onto it for the next 25 races and appeared to be headed for his first drivers' championship. But he suffered a neck injury at Kansas City in late September and was eventually forced to climb out of the car for the rest of the season and dropped to 18th overall.

With another 18th-place finish in 2003, and rankings of 21st and 26th the next two seasons, Marlin's tenure with Ganassi came to an end, and he selected MB2 from among several offers.

"This is an organization on the upswing," he said of his new team. "I still have some unfinished business as a driver, and that's why I am excited about joining MB2 Motorsports.

"And to drive a car with the same number that my father drove with, makes the move even more special."

Marlin gets some parking instructions from his pit crew teammates.

"I still have some unfinished business as a driver."

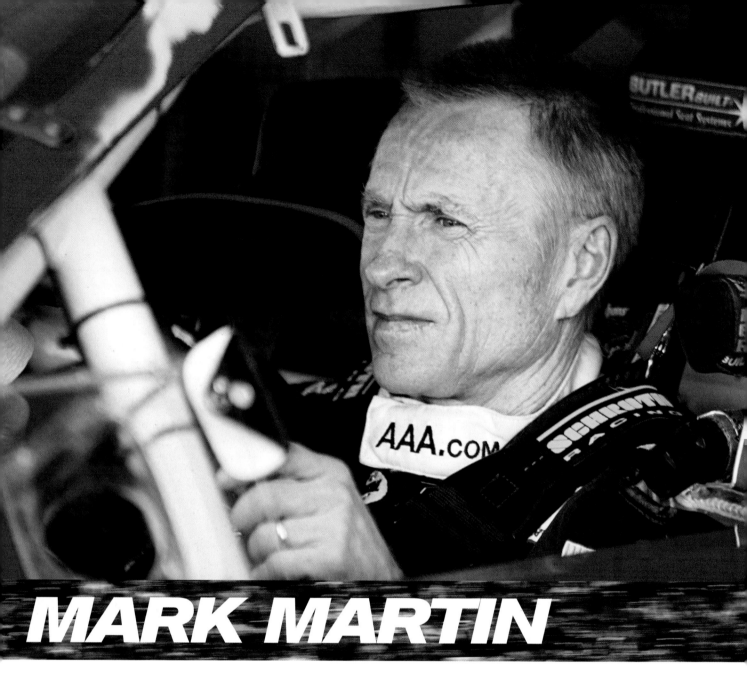

MARK MARTIN

NO. 6

BORN: January 9, 1959

HOMETOWN: Batesville, Ark.

TEAM: Roush Racing

CAR: Ford

SPONSOR: AAA

CUP WINS: 35

2005 CUP EARNINGS: $5,994,353

CAREER EARNINGS: $52 million

It may be a cliché, but Mark Martin lives it. He's not getting older, he's getting better.

Some people probably assumed the veteran from Batesville, Arkansas, was through when he finished 17th in the 2003 Winston Cup points standings, his worst result since he first climbed into Jack Roush's No. 6 car in 1988. Some people, including Martin himself, assumed he would be through at the end of 2005. That year was billed as his Salute To You tour, a grateful farewell season for the legion of NASCAR fans who had supported him and his old-school no-nonsense style since he arrived at NASCAR, running his own car, in 1981.

But by the end of 2005, not only had Martin finished fourth in the drivers' standings, mounted a very serious run at the championship and extended his consecutive-start streak to 579 races, he had agreed to Roush's request to spend one more year at the wheel.

And for the second successive year, he kept improving as the Nextel Cup season wore on. In 2004 he silenced critics by finishing fourth overall after breaking into the top 10 for the first time on the Labor Day weekend, just one week before the cut to the Chase.

In 2005 he advanced from ninth to fourth in the season's final seven races. He won the All-Star Challenge in May, but didn't win a points event until the 30th race of the year, when he took the checkers at Kansas City after leading

throughout the second half. That victory broke a 52-race winless streak.

"It wasn't the most exciting win of my career, but it was one well-deserved by my crew," said Martin.

Martin's crew, led by chief Pat Tryson, had stayed on for the Salute To You tour, out of loyalty, although other teams had tried to raid the team's personnel.

"That's one of the great honors I've had," Martin said late in the season. "I guess I'm just lucky. I can't be the most fun driver in the world to work with. I'm not a comedian. I put a lot of emphasis on effort, but not a lot on having fun."

But in the twilight of his career, he's a lot more fun than he once was. Regarded as aloof and serious-minded through most of his racing years, he has become warmer and far more approachable. And when he made a charge for the 2005 points title at the age of 46, he had millions of fans pulling for him to win it all, sometimes ahead of their own personal favorites.

Martin is often called the racer's racer, or the best stock car driver never to have won the Cup championship.

He has been the runner-up to the points winner four times (1990, 1994, 1998 and 2002) and lost the 1990 title to the late Dale Earnhardt by only 26 points. Another three times he finished third. His legion of followers, who

Arkansas native Mark Martin leading the pack at Phoenix in April 2006. He took 11th in the AAA-sponsored Ford.

love his commitment to traditional racing, the Roush team, and brush cuts, were ecstatic that he would return for 2006, because it meant one more opportunity to win it all.

Martin began racing cars competitively at the age of 15, "even before I had a driver's license." After apprenticing on the dirt tracks of Arkansas, he hit the asphalt of the American Speed Association and won the ASA crown three straight years, from 1978 through 1980. The next year he dabbled in NASCAR, entering his own car in the Winston Cup Series for five races, with top-10 finishes in two of them.

He ran a full season the next year and was ranked 14th overall, but had no major financing. So he sold his cars, raced a limited schedule for various teams, including four different owners in 1983 and left the Cup series completely in 1984 and 1985. He went back to his roots for the 1986 season, and won another ASA title. He was also working the Busch Grand National Series and has gone on to become the biggest winner in its history, running his victory total to a record 47 in 2005. It was during the 1987 Busch season that he got the attention of Roush, who was moving into Winston Cup racing the next year.

Martin was Roush's first driver and although

Martin began racing cars competitively at the age of 15, "even before I had a driver's license."

they didn't win in the inaugural year (their victory came late the next season at Rockingham), Martin had 10 top-10 finishes. The next year, the team finished third and has fallen out of the top 10 in only two seasons (2001 and 2003) since then. Martin calls Roush the best team owner in sport and considers him his surrogate father since his own father, Julian, died in a 1998 plane crash. So it was not surprising that when, encountering snags in landing a successor to the No. 6 car, Roush asked him to stay for one more season, Martin readily agreed.

And, as always he'll race to finish first.

"The first time I ever got in a Cup car back in 1981 at North Wilkesboro, I was there to win," he said before the 2005 season that was supposed to be his last.

"When we climb in that car at Homestead for the last race, I can guarantee you that we'll be looking to win that as well."

He lost that thrilling Homestead race to Greg Biffle by .017 seconds, the sixth-closest finish in Cup history. That epic duel would have been a great way to go out, had he indeed retired after 2005.

But millions of NASCAR fans are glad he didn't.

JEREMY MAYFIELD

For Jeremy Mayfield, the problem isn't getting there, it's making enough happen when he does.

The native of Owensboro, Kentucky, qualified for the elite 10 in each of the Chase's first two years, including a desperate, last-chance sprint to a berth in the playoff's inaugural season. But he stalled in the final dash to the drivers' title, finishing 10th in 2004 and ninth in 2005.

"We know how to get into the Chase," Mayfield concluded after the 2005 season. "It's a whole different deal, after you've gotten in, to win the championship in the last 10 races than it is in the first 26."

It was a tribute to both his judgment and his tenacity that Mayfield was able to urge the No. 9 Dodge even to 10th place in 2005. It was not a good year for the Chargers and when his driver won at Michigan in August, crew chief Slugger Labbe said the team "robbed the bank" because the car was of 20th-place caliber.

Although it was a gutsy decision by Labbe and Mayfield to gamble on a rapidly diminishing fuel supply for the final 52 laps that won them the Michigan race, Labbe was released in late October. The Michigan victory had given Evernham Motorsports a Cup win by two different drivers in the same season for the first time, but Ray Evernham was revamping his entire organization after overall ragged results.

NO. 19

BORN: May 27, 1969

HOMETOWN: Owensboro, Ky.

TEAM: Evernham Motorsports

CAR: Dodge

SPONSOR: Dodge Dealers

CUP WINS: 5

2005 CUP EARNINGS: $4,566,913

CAREER EARNINGS: $27.1 million

Kentucky's Jeremy Mayfield in the Dodge Charger 500.

Kenny Francis, the former crew chief, finished up the year in charge.

Mayfield started 2005 slowly and had only two top-10 finishes in the first 15 races, but his cars were finishing races cleanly. That helped him slip into the top 10 of the points standings to stay by the 18th race, a lot less dramatic process than the year before.

In 2004 Mayfield was 14th heading into the final qualifying race at Richmond and 55 points out of a Chase berth. But he won Richmond, to leapfrog into ninth place, and qualify by just 22 points. It was his first time in the top 10 since 1998, when he was driving for Roger Penske. But he endured four finishes of 30th or lower in the Chase to lose sight of the title.

In 2005, although he entered the Chase having completed the most laps (7,456), he logged only two top-10 finishes in the final 10 races.

Despite the flat endings, 2004 and 2005 at least got Mayfield back into Victory Lane. Before the dramatic triumph at Richmond, he hadn't celebrated a win since he took two races for Penske in 2000.

He got his only other career victory in his debut year with Penske. His first Cup win, at the Pocono 500 in June 1998, helped him to a career-high seventh place in the points standings. Evernham, in the early stages of building his Dodge partnerships, signed him to drive the No. 19 for the 2002 season after Mayfield had finished a disappointing 35th in 2001.

With Evernham, he's had consistent cars, despite the Charger's configuration problems in 2005. That has helped him emerge from the middle of the pack onto the edge of the driving elite.

Mayfield first started turning left at the age of 4, when his mini-motorcycle wore an oval

into the yard of his grandmother's house. He was racing BMX bikes at local tracks by the time he was 10, then moved into go-karts.

He moved into stock cars in the Street Stock Division at Kentucky Motor Speedway, winning enough there to graduate to Late Models. To pay the bills, he painted signs at Kentucky Speedway and in 1990, at the age of 19, he moved to Nashville to work as a fabricator at Sadler Racing.

Six months later, Earl Sadler gave him a Late Model to race. He competed in the ARCA Series and eventually was rookie of the year at Kentucky Motor Speedway. So, in October 1993, Sadler got him his Cup debut at Charlotte, where he was 29th, and agreed to provide him four more Cup rides in 1994. Cale Yarborough also gave him a dozen drives that year, and in 1995 Mayfield made his full-time debut for Yarborough, finishing 31st.

Yarborough released him after 23 races in 1996, and he finished that year, and raced all of 1997, for Michael Kranefuss. After the charismatic Mayfield finished 13th in the 1997 points standings, he moved to Penske for four seasons, and then on to Evernham.

A restructuring at Evernham has Mayfield excited about the future of the Dodge team. Mayfield, who once had 11 DNFs in a single season, had sliced those to just two by 2004 and only one in the disjointed 2005 season.

"We have learned a lot about what we need to be better," Mayfield says.

The Evernham pit crew go to work on Mayfield's Dodge in Darlington, May 2006. He finished the race 38th.

"It's a whole different deal, after you've gotten in, to win the championship in the last 10 races than it is in the first 26."

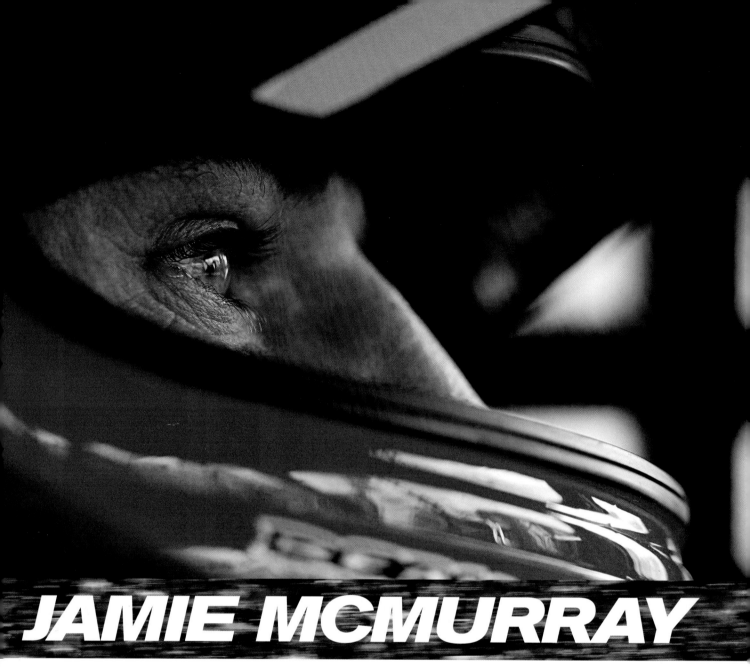

JAMIE MCMURRAY

NO. 26

BORN: June 3, 1976

HOMETOWN: Joplin, Mo.

TEAM: Roush Racing

CAR: Ford

SPONSORS: Irwin Tools, Sharpie, Crown Royal

CUP WINS: 1

2005 CUP EARNINGS: $3,923,968

CAREER EARNINGS: $12.5 million

The early feast had turned into a long famine for Jamie McMurray.

So the hungry young talent left Chip Ganassi Racing with Felix Sabates in search of a bigger meal. He turned to Roush Racing, which had a banquet of five drivers qualify for the 2005 Chase.

McMurray, a magnet for sponsors and fans, wasn't supposed to begin with Roush until the 2007 season, when he was slated to take over Mark Martin's No. 6, at Martin's request. But Kurt Busch's desire to leave Roush early resulted in McMurray inheriting the No. 97 in time for the 2006 season.

"I could have stayed another year, I really liked the people where I was," explained McMurray, one of the most respectful and level-headed drivers among the current class of Young Guns. "But I'd rather go to where I know my future is."

That future seemed to arrive in the fall of 2002, when McMurray was chosen for a full 2003 ride with Ganassi and also selected to sub the final six races of the 2002 season for the injured Sterling Marlin. A few weeks later, in his second career start, McMurray won at Charlotte. It was the first time in the modern era, and only the 11th time in Cup history, that a driver had won a points race within his first two starts.

"I won with Chip and Felix in our second race," McMurray recalls. "And it looked like a

very bright future. Unfortunately, it just didn't work out."

Although McMurray won rookie-of-the-year honors for Ganassi in 2003, by the time he left CGFS at the end of 2005, he had gone 114 races without a Cup victory.

He did pick up wins on other circuits, though, and is one of only a few NASCAR drivers to have won races in all three National series.

But McMurray got those wins in reverse of the usual order. Two weeks after grabbing his first Cup victory, he won his first Busch race at Atlanta, and then a week later got his second Busch victory at Rockingham. But it wasn't until 2004, racing for Ultra Motorsports at

Martinsville, that he earned his first Craftsman Truck checkered flag.

It was in the Trucks that McMurray made his first real impression on the national scene. While racing in NASCAR's RE/MAX Challenge Series, he made five Craftsman starts in 1999, then did a full schedule and finished 22nd in the 2000 truck standings.

McMurray got his start behind the wheel when he was eight years old, racing go-karts in Missouri. By the time he was 16, he had won four U.S. go-kart championships, represented the U.S.A. in a karting event in the former Soviet Union and captured the 1991 world championship. In karts, he toured in the rookie-junior class, at the same time current

Jamie McMurray (26) and Tony Stewart (20) in the Daytona 500 in 2006. The Roush Racing Ford of McMurray started the Big One in fine shape in sixth, but an accident put him back to a 37th-place finish.

McMurray during a pit stop in the 2006 Daytona 500 (left). Born in 1976, McMurrray is a former kart champ.

It was the first time in the modern era that a driver had won a points race within his first two starts.

Cup opponent Tony Stewart competed just above him in junior class.

In 1992 he moved up to late models, racing in the Grand American Late Model Class from 1996 to 1998. He ran NASCAR Dodge Weekly Series races at several tracks and captured the track championship at I-44 Speedway in 1997.

While competing in the Craftsman Truck Series in 2000, he also began racing in the Busch Series and finished third in the 2001 rookie-of-the-year standings. Besides his two wins late in 2002, he also had 17 Busch top-10s between 2000 and 2002.

Then he got his break subbing for Marlin and made the most of it. He won at Charlotte and had another top-five finish among the remaining six races of 2002.

In his first full year of Cup racing, McMurray was named the 2003 rookie of the year, ahead of Greg Biffle, and on the last weekend of the season won his first career pole. A year later he finished 11th, just missing the Chase in its inaugural year of operation. Although he didn't win a Nextel Cup race in 2004, McMurray was remarkably consistent, amassing 23 top-10

finishes, the second most in the premier series. Living up to his nickname of Mr. October, in the final 10 races of the season he collected eight top-10 finishes. He also won three times in just 14 starts on the Busch Series, and took home his first victory in the Truck series.

"We had four or five engines break on us," he said of his promising 2004 results. "Without those DNFs we probably would have made it into the Chase."

But 2005 was not a good season for McMurray, with Dodges struggling across the board. He did climb as high as seventh in the point standings after a runner-up finish at the Pepsi 400, but could manage only one top-10 placing in the next 14 races. He finished 12th overall in what would turn out to be his last season at Chip Ganassi Racing with Felix Sabates.

"After a whole bunch of dominos fell in place," he was able to leave Ganassi for Roush a year ahead of the original 2007 target.

"They've got really good drivers to learn from," McMurray said.

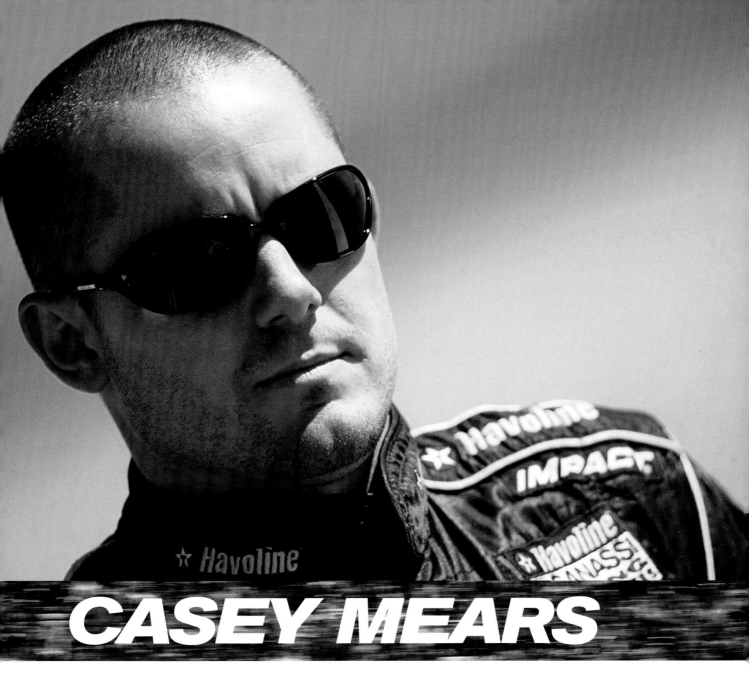

CASEY MEARS

His past was open wheel, his future is stock cars.

Presented with a variety of driving options in late 2001, Casey Mears, a member of a blueblood open-wheel racing family, consulted with his father Roger and his legendary uncle Rick about the direction his own career should take. Rick Mears was a four-time Indy 500 champion, and Roger also raced at Indy, but created his own legend as an off-road racer.

Casey Mears, whose background and lineage were almost all connected to open-wheel racing, had just driven in his first stock car race, finishing ninth in the final ARCA event of the year at Talladega. He could stay and continue a career which had promise in either the Indy Racing League or CART, or he could accept an offer from Welliver-Jessel Motorsports to run the 2002 Busch Series.

In the end, stock cars won out.

It hasn't been an easy initiation into the fendered fraternity. Although he's been improving each year, there was a point in 2004 when NASCAR pundits were wondering if Mears would be able to hang on to his job with Chip Ganassi and Felix Sabates. But that question was answered definitively late in the 2005 season when CGRFS announced it would add a fourth car, No. 42, to its stable beginning in 2006. And Casey Mears would drive it.

"It's cool the way it all worked out," Mears said.

NO. 42

BORN:
March 12, 1978

HOMETOWN:
Bakersfield, Calif.

TEAM: Ganassi Racing, Felix Sabates

CAR: Dodge

SPONSOR: Texaco

CUP WINS: 0

2005 CUP EARNINGS:
$4,234,171

CAREER EARNINGS:
$10.3 million

Casey Mears (41) t-bones Hermie Sadler in the 2005 Sharpie 500 at Bristol. Mears returned to the track after the incident and took 34th.

"We've had a couple of frustrating years, but I'd say 2005 was probably the most frustrating one because everything was there."

Mears was glad to have something work out, after a 2005 season filled with bad luck. He finished 22nd in the points race, the same as he had in 2004, but he could have been much higher. His team struggled with downforce, as most Dodge squads did, got into a hole early and was unable to dig itself out. But the second half was much better than the first and he ended with two top-five finishes in the last three races, and four top-10s in the last seven. His best result, however, was a fourth early in the year at Fort Worth, which looked like a strong bid for Victory Lane until a late caution got in the way.

"I could go down a long list of races where we were really fast, capable of top-five runs, and things out of our control happened," he told NASCAR.com.

"We've had a couple of frustrating years, but I'd say 2005 was probably the most frustrating one because everything was there."

Because it's a new entry, the No. 42 was to begin 2006 without provisional points, which makes qualifying in the early races critical. That was the downside to Mears' new ride, but the upside was far more important: continued

employment and a strong financial commitment from his owners and his sponsor.

Mears joined Ganassi for the 2003 Cup season, after finishing 21st in the 2002 Busch standings. He struggled through his rookie Cup season, with a whopping 10 DNFs and an overall 35th-place finish. He was also behind the wheel for 14 Busch races. But he did win his first stock car race that year, capturing the checkered flag at the ARCA event at Michigan in mid-June. Six weeks later he won ARCA races on back-to-back days at Pocono.

In 2004 his Cup season started strongly, and he won his first career pole at Pocono in August, following it up with his second successive pole at Indy – a career moment for a driver steeped in open-wheel history. (Mears says one of his strongest racing memories was watching his uncle Rick Mears pass Michael Andretti on turn four while winning his fourth Indy 500 title in 1991. Another was finishing fourth for Team Rahal in his first CART start in 2000 at California.)

But he couldn't take advantage of either pole, finishing 18th and 26th, respectively.

Mears had decided to pursue a NASCAR

career in 2001, but not before he was connected that season to another open-wheel legend. He replaced the horribly injured Alex Zanardi, and recorded two top-10 finishes in four CART starts before deciding upon stock cars as a future.

Stock car racing was a major departure from his past. Mears began racing BMX bicycles at the age of four, then switched to ATVs at his hometown speedway in Bakersfield, California. He climbed into go-karts in his early teens then moved into the SuperLites off-road series in1992. He competed in the Jim Russell USAC Triple Crown championship in 1993. When he won at Mesa Marin Raceway the following year, he was the second-youngest (16) winner in Triple Crown history. He finished third in the points standings, then won it all in 1995, at the age of 17.

Mears made his Indy Lites debut at Cleveland in 1996, finishing eighth, and drove in the series full-time in 1996. In 1999 he finished second in the points standings and became just the fourth driver to complete every lap in an Indy Lites season. In 2000 he won the Grand Prix of Houston, his first Indy Lites victory.

A year later, he was headed for stock car racing, and as 2006 opened he was in the No. 42 car in NASCAR's premier series.

"I think everybody is fired up about the new situation," he said.

Son of four-time Indy champ Rick Mears, Casey started racing stock cars in ARCA and chose fendered racing over the IRL and CART.

JOE NEMECHEK

NO. 01

BORN: September 26, 1963

HOMETOWN: Lakeland, Fla.

TEAM: MB2 Motorpsorts

CAR: Chevrolet

SPONSOR: U.S. Army

CUP WINS: 4

2005 CUP EARNINGS: $4,223,376

CAREER EARNINGS: $23.5 million

Sometimes Joe Nemechek must feel that if he didn't have bad luck, he wouldn't have any luck at all.

In 2002 and 2003 Nemechek had one team (Haas-Carter) withdraw from Cup action during the season, another (Hendrick Motorsports) release him over sponsorship problems and a third (MB2) give him a ride only until their injured driver (Jerry Nadeau) was able to get back behind the wheel.

And his 2005 season was filled with the kind of misfortune that makes drivers wonder if the racing gods are conspiring against them.

It appears that Nemechek is now entrenched at MB2, and not just because Nadeau's injuries may prevent his return to competition.

Nemechek finished 16th in the 2005 drivers' standings, his second-best ranking in his dozen Cup years. But the No. 01 U.S. Army Chevrolet could have gone much higher, perhaps even qualified for the Chase, had a few breaks gone its way.

"It seemed like we had some terrible luck in a lot of races," Nemechek understated.

In the season's second race at California, Nemechek was leading but blew an engine with 77 laps to go. So, despite leading more laps than any other car, the No. 01 finished 39th. The next race, at Las Vegas, he was in third when he took on a bad set of tires in the last pit stop, was nearly lapped and dropped to 19th. A week later at Atlanta, he had climbed

as high as second, but a hole in his radiator ended his day with 45 laps to go.

"That's racing," Nemechek says, invoking the mantra of all drivers. "You continue to battle on and never quit."

He did just that, and in the Coca-Cola 600 at Lowe's Raceway on Memorial Day weekend, he led for more than 20 laps with just 10 laps to go. But he ran over a piece of car debris and sliced his right-rear tire, which sent him into the outside wall. A fairly certain win turned into an 18th place finish.

And there were another half-dozen races when he was heading toward a top-10 finish before some form of bad luck befell him.

"When you're out there dominating races, then all of a sudden, something happens … man that's pretty hard to fix," Nemechek told his hometown paper in Lakeland, Florida.

As 2004 ended, it seemed like 2005 was going to be a breakthrough season. But misfortune was riding shotgun and, given the recurring mishaps, a 16th-place finish was quite commendable.

Nemechek is known as Front Row Joe because of his tendency to qualify for good positions on the starting grid. Wally Dallenbach, his teammate with the Felix Sabates organization, gave Nemechek the nickname at Pocono in 1997, and it stuck.

That Nemechek usually qualifies well comes as a bit of a surprise, considering that

"Front Row Joe" Nemechek usually starts a race in good shape in Cup events, but then luck seems to run out as the race continues.

Starting ninth at Dover in September 2005, Nemechek clipped the wall but came back to place 17th in the U.S. Army Monte Carlo.

"That's racing. You continue to battle on and never quit."

he started racing much later than other top drivers. He took up competitive motocross at the age of 13 and stayed on the two-wheelers for six years, bringing home more than 300 trophies.

When Nemechek moved into stock cars, it took only four years before he began a stunning streak of three straight years in which he won both the rookie of the year and the drivers' championship in three different series. He took the double crown in Southeastern Mini-Stocks in 1987, in the United Stock Car Alliance in 1988 and in the All-Pro Series in 1989.

By 1990 he was ready for NASCAR and broke into the Busch series where, of course, he was named rookie of the year. In 1992, driving the family-owned car, Nemechek beat Bobby Labonte to win the Busch drivers' championship by only three points, the narrowest margin in the history of NASCAR's three major national series.

Nemechek and wife Andrea kept their car in the Busch Series but also tried three Cup races in 1993, and he ran two more for Morgan-McClure the same year. Larry Hendrick hired him for the Winston Cup in 1994 and he

had three top-10s, while finishing 27th in the points standing – good for third in the rookie-of-the-year race.

For the next two years, Nemechek ran his own car in the Winston Cup, but finished 28th and 34th, so when Sabates offered him a ride for 1997, he took it. While he didn't win a race that year, he did take two poles and was in the front row five times.

In 1999, his third and final year with Sabates, he finished only 34th but won his first Cup race, at New Hampshire where he'd made his premier series debut six years earlier.

From there, it was two seasons with Andy Petree, which included a victory at Rockingham in 2001. Then came the unsettling 2002 and 2003 seasons, although there was a victory for Hendrick at Richmond in 2003.

Driving for MB2 in 2004, he finished just 36th in the points standings as six DNFs marred the season, but he closed strongly with six top-10s in the last 10 races, including a Busch-Nextel sweep at Kansas Speedway. That indicated the No. 01 was peaking for a strong 2005.

But while he had the car and the skill, Nemechek just didn't have the luck.

RYAN NEWMAN

Wherever there's a pole, Ryan Newman is probably revving his engine nearby.

In 2005 Newman won his fourth consecutive Bud Pole Award, presented to the Nextel Cup driver who starts the most races in the No. 1 position. He qualified fastest for eight different races, twice as many as any other driver. And that was his lowest total in three years.

Although he is sometimes called Mr. Friday, the native Indianan does his fair share of great racing on Sundays too. In 2003, for instance, he won eight Cup races, the most in the series.

But Newman, who holds a degree in Vehicle Structural Engineering from Purdue University, hasn't found the long-term consistency – from qualifying trim to race trim; from first race to last – needed to capture a Nextel drivers' title.

He's certainly nibbled around the edges. In 2005 he finished sixth for the third time in four years. The other time, he was seventh.

Until 2005, the big hurdle between Newman and the honored seat at the year-end banquet was finishing what he started.

"Every year, having fewer DNFs is our goal," Newman said in late 2005. "This year, we've accomplished our goal."

Newman had only three DNFs in 2005, one-third of the previous season's total. And his 16 top-10s were up from the 14 he had in 2004. But he had to wait until the 27th race of the season, the first event of the Chase at

NO. 12

BORN:
December 8, 1977

HOMETOWN:
South Bend, Ind.

TEAM:
Penske South

CAR: Dodge

SPONSORS: ALLTEL, Mobil One

CUP WINS: 12

2005 CUP EARNINGS:
$5,578,114

CAREER EARNINGS:
$23.8 million

Ryan Newman leads a pack of cars at the 2006 Daytona 500. He finished third, behind Jimmie Johnson and Casey Mears.

Opposite: Newman celebrates winning the MBNA at Dover, September 2004.

New Hampshire, to claim his only victory of the year. By then, he already had five poles and another four starts in the front row.

Ironically, he started from the 13 spot when he won at Loudon.

The No. 12 car, like most of the Dodge Chargers, fought against aerodynamic problems all season, mostly related to the nose configuration. Battling his car as well as his opponents, Newman's driving was actually better than his results indicated.

Although he qualifies fast, he often starts the season slow, which cost him a chance at the drivers' championship in 2003, when he won eight races. In 2005 he lingered in the lower middle of the top 10 all season, but needed an eighth in the 26th race to qualify for the 10th and final berth in the Chase. After following his Loudon win with a fifth and a fourth, he moved all the way up to second in the points

standings, but a 23rd at Kansas City, put him out of the hunt.

"We know we struggled this year, and we're going to try to have the right tools to do what we need to do in 2006," Newman said.

Most drivers would be happy to "struggle" to sixth place overall but Newman sets the bar for himself very high.

Newman's parents started him in Quarter Midget cars before he was 5, and he eventually became a member of the sport's hall of fame. In 1993, at 15, he was All-American Midget Series rookie of the year, and series champion. He later took top rookie honors in the USAC National Midgets (1995), Silver Crown (1996) and Sprint cars (1999). When he won the USAC Silver Bullet national championship in 1999, with 12 top-10 finishes in just 15 races, it helped him land a stock car ride in ARCA for 2000. He won in his second start, took a

couple of other checkered flags and in November, Roger Penske gave him his first Cup start at Phoenix. There, he ran into engine problems and finished 41st overall.

In 2001, in what Newman called "my ABC experience" he raced twice in ARCA, 15 times in the Busch Series and started seven Cup races. He won at Michigan in his ninth Busch start and grabbed six poles. It took only three Cup starts to land his first pole, at the Coca-Cola 600, tying Mark Martin's record for earliest pole in a career.

That set the table for his impressive full-season debut for Penske in 2002, when Newman edged Jimmie Johnson in one of the tightest rookie-of-the-year battles in NASCAR history. He tied Martin for the series lead of 22 top-10 finishes, establishing a new Cup rookie record. His six poles were one better than Davey Allison's rookie record. The break-

through season was heralded by a victory in the non-points, but prestigious, all-star event in May; and in September at Loudon, New Hampshire, he won his first Cup race.

"It was an unbelievable season," Newman said.

He followed up with a phenomenal eight wins in 2003, but finished sixth in points because of seven DNFs, mostly early in the season. Nine DNFs marred an otherwise excellent 2004, when he finished seventh.

Despite growing up in Indiana, the heart of American open-wheel racing, Newman's dream was to win the Daytona 500. He was seventh in his 2002 debut at stock car racing's premier event, but since then hasn't finished better than 20th. But there are few NASCAR fans who don't believe that one day Newman will take the checkered flag at the famous oval.

After taking the pole, of course.

KYLE PETTY

It says everything about this third generation NASCAR mainstay that Kyle Petty hadn't won a Cup race in a decade, and had only two top-10 finishes in the previous three years, but was still chosen as a finalist for *Sports Illustrated*'s 2005 Sportsman of the Year.

He carries a last name that can be a beacon or a burden, depending on how it's handled.

But while Kyle Petty hasn't won the races that his famous father, Richard "The King" Petty, or his grandfather, Lee Petty, did, he has more than lived up to the family's honorable tradition.

Kyle Petty cares. He cares about the fans who watch him race, which is why he's been so disappointed in his on-track performance in recent seasons.

He cares about the future of his sport, which is why he was the only team leader to put his own version of NASCAR's extremely controversial prototype "Car of Tomorrow" onto the Daytona track during 2006 test week.

He cares about humanity, which is why, in 2004, he and his wife Pattie opened Victory Junction Gang Camp for chronically ill children from across the country. The family had already been named "persons of the year" by NASCAR in 2000. Petty also works with the Boy Scouts of America and the Make-A-Wish Foundation; created the Race to End Hunger; and founded his Charity Ride Across America,

NO. 45

BORN:
June 20, 1960

HOMETOWN:
Trinity, N.C.

TEAM: Petty Enterprises

CAR: Dodge

SPONSOR:
Wells Fargo

CUP WINS: 8

2005 CUP EARNINGS:
$3,465,687

CAREER EARNINGS:
$24 million

The third generation of NASCAR's first family, Kyle Petty, shown here in the Allstate 400 at the Brickyard in 2005, was Sports Illustrated's 2005 Sportsman of the Year for his work with critically ill children.

which has raised over $1.5 million since 1995.

That's a full plate for any person, but Petty also runs the day-to-day operations of Petty Enterprises, owned by his father. And he's a pretty good stock car driver too, although recent results don't reflect that.

Petty is ranked 26th in victories in Cup racing's modern era, and 16th on the all-time money list. There is no arguing that he's run into dry times in the new millennium: his 27th overall finish in 2005 was his best since he was 22nd in 2002. He also had a pair of top-10 finishes in 2005, which he hadn't done since he racked up nine of them in 1999.

Although there are always rumors that he will retire to concentrate on running the family business, as he entered the 2006 season Petty felt things were on the upswing for his No. 45 car. He had hired Bobby Labonte to drive the No. 43, giving him an accomplished veteran

teammate on the track. And Robbie Loomis, Jeff Gordon's former crew chief, was brought in to be vice-president of operations.

"It's a huge challenge to get that car back to Victory Lane," Loomis said. "But we'll just put our best foot forward."

Petty had finished 33rd, with a whopping nine DNFs in 2004, a 37th in 2003, and a 43rd in 2001, so maybe the improvement to 27th in 2005 and the additions of Labonte and Loomis might inch him back toward the top 15.

Petty is a multi-talented individual who runs distance races (he appeared in the 2006 Disney World Marathon, wearing bib 4545), had a good opportunity to become a country singer and was offered scholarships to play college baseball.

But if you're a Petty, stock car driving is in your blood. When he was only two months old, Petty was at his first Daytona race with his

parents. Growing up, he worked at the family garage in North Carolina, learning about the racing business from every viewpoint.

While he was still 18 years old, Petty won the ARCA 200, and Richard Petty put him in five Cup races that same 1979 season. In his debut at Talladega, he finished a strong ninth.

In 1980 he was third in the rookie-of-the-year standings, and raced four more years for the family firm, finishing between 12th and 16th.

He moved to the Wood Brothers in 1985 and had five excellent seasons, moving up to ninth in the drivers' standings in his first season there and being named comeback driver of the year. When he won his first Winston Cup race at Richmond in 1986, the Pettys became the first family in NASCAR history to record victories from three different generations. He won at Charlotte the next year and finished seventh overall, but two years later he joined newcomer Felix Sabates' SABCO team.

After a rough 30th finish in their first year together, Sabates and Petty jumped to 11th in the standings in 1990, won at North Wilkesboro, and recorded 14 top-10 finishes. Sabates was so excited by the victory that he gave Petty a Rolls-Royce to thank him.

Petty spent eight seasons with Sabates, with superb back-to-back campaigns in 1992 and 1993, resulting in a pair of fifth places in the standings, three victories and a combined 18 top-fives. Overall, he won six times for Sabates but, after regressing to 30th and 27th, he came back to the family-owned team in 1997.

He had nine top-10s in 1997 and again in 1999, but wasn't winning races, and after finishing 15th in the points standings in his first year back at Petty Enterprises, he slipped to 30th and 26th the next two years.

In 2000 the Pettys had to live a parent's worst nightmare when their 19-year-old son Adam was killed during a Busch Series race at New Hampshire. The family was devastated, but Richard and Kyle decided to carry on the business and out of respect for his son, Kyle moved from his No. 44 Cup car and into Adam's No. 45 for the remainder of the Busch Series.

He still drives No. 45 and has intensified what had already been a full schedule of charity work.

Petty's cars haven't performed as well as he hoped, and he has often said he wants to move up in the standings just to bring a little more light into the worlds of the fans who sit in the stands, wearing Kyle Petty t-shirts.

Every one of those fans understands exactly why a driver who didn't win a race could be nominated for Sportsman of the Year.

Car testing at Lowe's Motor Speedway in May 2006, behind Mark Martin. The 46-year-old Petty has eight Cup wins.

"It's a huge challenge to get that car back to Victory Lane," Loomis said. *"But we'll just put our best foot forward."*

ELLIOTT SADLER

NO. **38**

BORN: **April 30, 1975**

HOMETOWN: **Emporia, Va.**

TEAM: **Robert Yates Racing**

CAR: **Ford**

SPONSOR: **M&M's**

CUP WINS: **3**

2005 CUP EARNINGS: **$5,024,119**

CAREER EARNINGS: **$24.4 million**

A race career, just like a race car, can stall even when it seems to be running smoothly and quickly.

So, Elliott Sadler hopes that the 2005 Nextel Cup season was merely a case of taking that one step back before taking at least two more forward. After winning twice in 2004, qualifying sixth for the inaugural Chase, and finishing ninth overall, Sadler didn't pick up a win – or earn a Chase berth – in 2005.

With the No. 38 car struggling in the second half, Sadler's owner, Robert Yates Racing, switched crew chiefs in late September. Todd Parrott moved over to Dale Jarrett, and engineer Kevin Buskirk took over as Sadler's interim crew chief.

"It was a tough season," Sadler said simply.

It didn't start out that way, as Sadler was building upon his career-best 2004 season, when he reached the top 10 for the first time. In five previous seasons, he had never been better than the 22nd he recorded in 2003, his first year with RYR.

Through the first 16 races in 2005, Sadler stood third in the points standing, two spots higher than he was at the same point in the previous season. And he'd climbed into the top three despite only one top-five finish (second at Bristol, where he also won the pole). But he was doing exactly what he wanted, "coming in under the radar" the whole race and grabbing dozens of important points in the process. In

eight of the first 16 races, he was in the top 10.

But then the double-figure finishes began to pile up, and when he finished only 17th at Richmond, the last qualifying race, it wasn't good enough to qualify for the Chase. He stood 11th for a playoff that could have only 10 candidates and eventually slid to 13th overall.

While 2005 was clearly a disappointment for Sadler and RYR, it did signal that his impressive improvement the year before was no fluke. After finishing 22nd in the points standing for Yates in 2003, Sadler was a contender in almost every race of 2004, other than the final handful of the inaugural Chase when terrible results dropped him from fourth to ninth.

Sadler opened the 2004 season on fire, with three top-10 finishes in the first five races, and his second career victory in the April race at Texas. It was the first victory in 14 months for a RYR car and ended a drought of more than three years for Sadler. He won by just 0.02 seconds over Kasey Kahne in what was then the eighth-closest race in NASCAR history. That put a quick end to the good-natured ribbing Sadler had been taking from other drivers about his inability to cash in on his obvious talent.

Then, a few months later at California, Sadler did it again, winning the Pop Secret 500, after starting 17th in the grid. That victory, with one more qualifier to go before the 10-race countdown to the title, guaranteed him a spot in NASCAR's first Chase.

Elliott Sadler (38) in practice at Martinsville in March 2006, with Jeremy Mayfield. The popular M&M's Ford driver took sixth.

Sadler spinning out in turn 4 during the 2003 UAW-GM Quality 500 at Lowe's.

"To clinch a spot, not by just riding around and finishing, but by actually winning a race is fantastic," the jubilant Sadler said. "This is a dream come true. This is what I came to this team to drive this car for. We're California dreaming."

Sadler had come to Yates to win, which is why enduring the entire 2005 season without a victory was so disappointing.

Sadler arrived at RYR in 2003 after four rather average years with the Wood Brothers, in which he won just one race (at Bristol in March 2001), had only three other top-fives and never finished higher than 23rd in the points standings. His first year at Yates, he improved only to 22nd and had just two top-fives, but he did start to exhibit what would be his long-term strength when he harvested nine top-10 finishes, the most of his career. He struggled to finish races, though, with nine DNFs, which he cut to one in 2004 and two in 2005.

Like many drivers, Sadler, the younger brother of NASCAR driver Hermie Sadler, got his first driving experience in go-karts. He started at the age of seven, and at eight won the 1983–84 Virginia State championship. By the time he moved to stock cars, he had won more than 200 kart races.

"To clinch a spot, not by just riding around and finishing, but by actually winning a race is fantastic."

Sadler was only 18 when he ran his first full season in NASCAR's Dodge Weekly series. Two years later he took the track championship at Boston Speedway, winning six races in a row en route to a 13-victory season. That year, and the next one, he also ran a limited Busch Series schedule before graduating to NASCAR's second-best series full-time in 1997.

Sadler made quite a splash in Busch racing, winning the pole at Daytona in the season opener of his rookie year. In just his 13th Busch start, at Nazareth, he won his first NASCAR national series race and went on to win two more races on the way to a fifth-place finish in the Busch standings. By the time he moved into Cup racing with the Wood Brothers in 1999, he had won five races, collected five poles and gathered 12 top-five finishes in just 76 Busch starts.

He stayed with the Wood Brothers for four years, before moving to RYR to replace the departing legend, Ricky Rudd, in 2003. It wasn't a great debut year, but toward the end of the season Yates installed Todd Parson as crew chief and the roots of a successful team began to take hold. The team leapt to ninth in 2004 and, despite the slide to 13th in 2005, the No. 38 car has served notice that it will be a long-term contender.

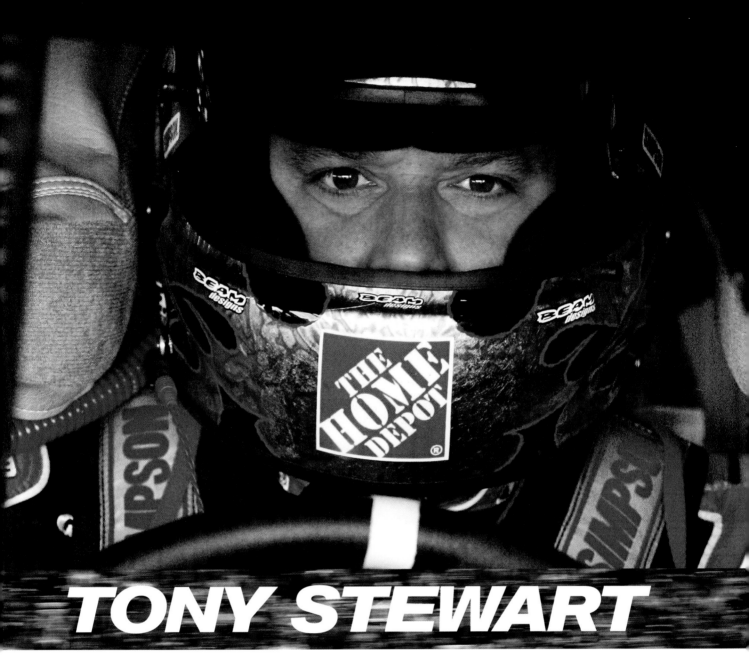

TONY STEWART

Following the path of so many of the great drivers before him – including his close friend Dale Earnhardt Sr. – Tony Stewart has elevated himself from "bad boy" to fan favorite.

Stewart was seen as somewhat of a hard-edged villain when he won the points championship in 2002. He had frequent emotional blowups and twice was involved in altercations with cameramen. Two years later, he shoved Brian Vickers in the chest after a race, knocking the breath out of the rookie driver.

But when he won the Nextel Cup again in 2005, riding a tidal wave of consistency, Stewart was a changed man. Still a fierce competitor

on the pavement, he was kinder and gentler off it. He was getting along better with the other drivers – even accepting compliments from once-bitter rival Jeff Gordon – relationships were smooth with his crew and he was even reaching out to fans, developing a new fence-climbing routine to communicate with them when he won a race.

After what has been called his "tortured" run to the 2002 Winston Cup title, other drivers such as Dale Jarrett and Mark Martin talked to him, with the biggest influence probably being Mike Wallace, who told him he was letting distractions get in the way of his accomplishments. The turning point, however, came when team owner Joe Gibbs called Stewart

NO. 20
BORN: May 20, 1971
HOMETOWN:
Rushville, Ind.
TEAM:
Joe Gibbs Racing
CAR: Chevrolet
SPONSOR:
Home Depot
CUP WINS: 24
2005 CUP EARNINGS:
$6,987,535
CAREER EARNINGS:
$41.8 million

The Champ at Texas in April 2006. Tony Stewart, the Indiana native with more than $40 million in Cup earnings, took third in the Samsung/Radio Shack 500 after starting in 40th spot.

Opposite: A former open-wheel driver, Stewart has emerged as one of NASCAR's most dominant drivers.

into the garage during the off-season between 2004 and 2005, to talk with his crew, hoping to make the talented, but often anger-riddled, driver realize just how difficult his outbursts were making their jobs. Stewart said later he wasn't sure that Gibbs was going to retain his services.

But Stewart altered his actions and didn't have any untoward incidents in 2005, while streaking to the points lead in mid-season and hanging onto it most of the way home.

"I put this team through hell," Stewart said in the 2005 victory celebration. "I didn't have a good feeling after the first championship because of what had happened during that season. But the team never gave up on me."

In fact, no current driver-crew chief duo has been together longer than Stewart and Greg Zipadelli, his crew chief. Zipadelli told Stewart at the end of the 2004 season that his attitude was hurting the team and Stewart, jolted, straightened up.

But while the team was getting along well, as late as the Pocono mid-June race, when he was 29th and had fallen to 10th in the drivers' standings, Stewart was calling 2005 "probably the worst season we'd ever had." The No. 20 had finished second three times but hadn't

won since the previous August. It didn't look like the Sonoma race in late June was going to be any better when he lost fourth gear and was on his way to losing third gear.

But holding the car in gear with one hand and steering with the other, he passed Ricky Rudd and won.

That started an incredible run of four victories in six races, which propelled Stewart into first place, a spot he never fully relinquished for the rest of the season.

Among those four victories was his first restrictor plate triumph at Daytona, in which he had the pole and led the entire race, other than pit stops. Afterward, he spontaneously climbed the flag stand right to the top.

"You just don't have nights like that very often," Stewart explained. "I'm too old and fat to do that." But his fans now expect some kind of ascent after a win.

A month later, Stewart, who was born and raised in Columbus, Indiana, less than an hour south of Indianapolis, realized a lifelong dream. He won the Brickyard 400, his first win at Indianapolis Motor Speedway in 15 attempts, in three different racing series.

"If I were to die tomorrow, I'd die happy," he said of the emotional victory.

*"I put this team
through hell,"
Stewart said in
the 2005 victory
celebration.*

Stewart had moved back to Indiana before the season after six years in North Carolina, and that had a settling effect on him. He had begun his racing career there a quarter-century earlier, and won his first race in 1980 at the Columbus Faigrounds. He won an International Karting Federation championship in 1983, and by 1987, at the age of 16, he was World Karting Association national champion.

Stewart was encouraged by his father Nelson, who owned the karts and was his crew chief. "He never let me settle for second," the son recalls, a theme that is still with him.

He was into Three-Quarter Midgets by 1989, graduated to the USAC ranks in 1991 and was named rookie of the year, before going on to win the USAC National Midget title in 1994 and the USAC Triple Crown – National Midget, Spring and Silver Crown – in 1995, which had never before been accomplished.

That success elevated Stewart to the IRL, where he won the rookie-of-the-year crown in 1996, and the entire series title the next year. He dabbled in closed-wheel racing that year too, running nine Busch Series races for Ranier/Walsh Racing. He was a very hot property and Joe Gibbs vowed he'd bring him over from open wheel and into NASCAR.

He ran five Busch races for Gibbs in 1997 and 22 in 1998.

While running a full IRL schedule, Stewart won three Busch Series races for Gibbs and rookie-of-the-year title in 1998, and became the first person to complete the Indianapolis 500 and Coca-Cola 600 on the same day, with excellent ninth- and fourth-place finishes, respectively.

He was a full-time Winston Cup driver by 1999, and won the rookie-of-the-year title, finishing fourth overall with three wins. He won six the next year, but five DNFs kept him down at sixth place. He'd moved up to second by 2001, and in 2002 he took the Winston Cup title by 31 points over Mark Martin, and also won $9,163,761, the third highest total in NASCAR history.

After a 2004 season in which he entered the Chase in fourth, dropped to sixth, and had his heart-to-heart talks with his owner and crew chief, Stewart won his 2005 title by 36 points, roughly the same margin by which he'd won his first crown three years earlier. But this was a different Tony Stewart than the champion of 2002.

"It's nice that they don't have to talk about my behavior anymore," he said.

BRIAN VICKERS

Brian Vickers likes to do things in a hurry, which is a pretty handy trait for a stock car driver.

He became the youngest Busch Series champion in NASCAR history when he captured three races and was in the top 10 a clockwork-like 21 times on the way to the 2003 points title. He did not turn 20 years of age until late that season.

He had the second biggest season-to-season improvement in the 2005 Nextel Cup standings, jumping to 17th from 25th the year before.

He won six races against the men of NASCAR's Weekly Racing Series, when he was just 16 years old.

The "can't miss" tag has been stapled to Vick-ers' racing suit since he was in his early teens, even if his mercurial rise was slightly slowed by his first two years on the Nextel Cup circuit. He didn't land a win in his first 77 starts, although he came achingly close at Pocono in June 2005. Carl Edwards got by him with 28 laps to go, relegating Vickers to second.

Vickers did win the 2005 Nextel Open at Charlotte, a huge thrill for a native of North Carolina. But the ultra-talented young driver admits that there is a steep learning curve in the sport's top series.

"I thought it wouldn't be that much different than the Busch Series," he said to reporters after his rookie year of 2004. "You think you've done this before and been to most of the tracks

NO. 25

BORN:
October 24, 1983

HOMETOWN:
Thomasville, N.C.

TEAM: Hendrick Motorsports

CAR: Chevrolet

SPONSOR: GMAC

CUP WINS: 0

2005 CUP EARNINGS:
$3,982,133

CAREER EARNINGS:
$7.3 million

The youngest Busch Series champ ever, Brian Vickers got into a Cup car in 2004 driving for Hendrick Motorsports. Here he practices for the 2005 Sony HD 500.

"To the other competitors, I was just another driver."

and it wouldn't be any big deal. But the difference between Busch and Cup is everything."

Vickers was still languishing in 24th place when he had the heart-breaking loss to Edwards at Pocono. But from there he and his crew really picked up the pace, and had it not been for a poor November, when he finished 19th, 26th and 43rd, Vickers could have cracked the top 15 in points.

To move into the elite circle, Vickers knows he has to improve his performances on short tracks. He had just one top-15 finish in short-track races in 2005. But Vickers feels that spending the entire season getting into synch again with crew chief Lance McGrew will pay big dividends. They won the 2003 Busch title together, before Vickers graduated to Cup racing with chief Peter Sospenzo in 2004. Owner Rick Hendrick moved Sospenzo over to Terry Labonte, so that Vickers and McGrew could be reunited in 2005. With all new cars, the pair took a while to get back in the groove, but hit their stride in the summer.

"We were behind the eight ball the whole

season," Vickers said. "We had to get used to each other again."

In 2005 Vickers had five top-five finishes and another five in the top 10. But that first Cup victory eluded him. Still, the team is headed decisively in the right direction, moving up from just four top-10 finishes in 2004, none of those in the top five.

Although he grew up in a state dominated by Lowe's Motor Speedway, Vickers says that his first choices of a site to win a race would be the historic tracks at Indianapolis, Daytona or Darlington. When he was young, Vickers and his family spent the last week of December with his family at the Daytona KartWeek.

Vickers began racing go-karts at the age of 10 and said it "wasn't until a few years later that I realized there was the potential to make a career out of racing."

That potential included four North Carolina State go-kart championships and three national championships before his 15th birthday. Then he moved into the Allison Legacy Car Series and rang up five wins, before gradu-

ating to Late Models in NASCAR's Weekly Racing Series in 1999, when he was turning 16.

"To the other competitors, I was just another driver," said Vickers.

But he was anything but just another driver to NASCAR talent scouts. In 2000 he joined the Hooter's ProCup Series, was rookie of the year and became the youngest race winner in series history. He finished second in ProCup points the next year and also made it into four Busch Series races.

Vickers made 21 more Busch starts with a family-owned team in 2002, a season that saw him qualify for Charlotte's race on a Friday morning, then hurry home for his high-school graduation ceremonies on Friday night, and then return to Charlotte to race on Saturday. But he was forced to miss his high-school prom that spring because he was racing at Bristol. His racing got stronger as the season

progressed, "which made me hungry for 2003."

That hunger would soon be partially satisfied. After the 2002 season, Hendrick Motorsports signed Vickers for the '03 Busch Series. Eleven months and three wins later, at the age of 20, he became the youngest points champion in Busch history. He also made his Cup debut with five races that season and, although he finished no higher than 13th, in four of his starts he was among the top five qualifiers.

He moved up to a full Cup schedule in 2004, still qualifying better than he finished, with 11 top-five starts including his first two career poles, at Richmond and California, on the way to a 25th place standing.

He put the experience of his rookie year to use in 2005, jumping to 17th overall and signaling that the No. 25 car is clearly on the rise.

Vickers (25), Mears (42) and Marlin (14) in some close action in the 2006 Daytona 500. The North Carolina native started 35th and ran well, placing seventh.

CLINT BOWYER

NO. 07

BORN: May 30, 1979

HOMETOWN:
Emporia, Kan.

TEAM: Childress Racing

CAR: Chevrolet

SPONSOR:
Jack Daniel's

- Bowyer finished second in the 2005 Busch Series standings, 68 points behind Martin Truex Jr. in a season-long battle that came down to the final race. He had two victories and 12 top-five finishes, and won $1,397,840.

- He won the 2002 NASCAR Weekly Racing Series midwest championship with 10 wins and 18 top-five finishes in 19 starts in the Modified division at Lakeside Speedway in Kansas City.

- Richard Childress entered Bowyer in one 2005 Nextel Cup race, in April at Phoenix. He started 25th and finished 22.

DENNY HAMLIN

NO. 11

BORN:
November 18, 1980

HOMETOWN:
Chesterfield, Va.

TEAM: Joe Gibbs Racing

CAR: Chevrolet

SPONSOR:
Federal Express

- Hamlin made seven Nextel Cup starts in the latter part of 2005, and had three top-10s.

- In his sixth Cup start, at Phoenix in November 2005, he won his first pole.

- He raced in the Busch Series in 2005, with one top-5 and 11 top-10s.

- In 2004 Hamlin had 10 wins in the Late Model Challenge Series at four different tracks.

- In 2003 he became the only driver in Southampton Motor Speedway history to win four consecutive 200-lap races.

TODD KLUEVER

- Kluever may take over Mark Martin's No. 6 car for Roush Racing in 2007. Scheduled to run selected Busch Series and selected Nextel Cup races in 2006.

- In 2005 he was the highest-ranked rookie in Craftsman Trucks, finishing 11th, with six top-five results.

- He won Roush Racing's "Race for the Ride" (nicknamed the "Gong Show") in November 2004.

- In 2001, Kluever was the Midwest All-Racing Series champion and rookie of the year, and was also Madison International Speedway Champion.

Busch Series 2006
BORN: July 6, 1978
HOMETOWN:
Sun Prairie, Wis.
TEAM:
Roush Racing

TRAVIS KVAPIL

- Kvapil was one of only two Nextel Cup rookies with full-time rides in 2005, racing for Penske in the No. 77 car, with two top-10 finishes and a 33rd-place ranking.

- In 2003 he won the Craftsman Trucks points championship for Xpress Motorsports, coming from third before the final race to first overall. He had one win and 22 top-10s.

- In four seasons in Craftsman Trucks, he had five race victories, 64 top-10s and never finished outside the top 10 in the drivers' championship.

- He was rookie of the year at Madison International Speedway in 1995 and won the Late Model track championship in 1996.

NO. 32
BORN:
March 1, 1976
HOMETOWN:
Jamesville, Wis.
TEAM:
PPI Motorsports
CAR: Chevrolet
SPONSOR: Tide

SCOTT RIGGS

NO. 10
BORN: Jan 1, 1971
HOMETOWN:
Bahama, N.C.
TEAM:
Evernham
Motorsports
CAR: Dodge
SPONSOR: Valvoline,
Stanley Tools

- Riggs finished 35th in the 2004 Nextel Cup standings and 36th in 2005, with two top-fives and four top-10s.

- In 2005 he won his first Cup pole at Martinsville in April and finished a career-high second at Michigan in August.

- He won five races in the 2001 NASCAR Craftsman Truck Series

- Riggs was the 2002 Busch Series rookie of the year, with two wins and eight top-fives.

PAUL TRACY

Busch Series
BORN:
December 17, 1968
HOMETOWN:
Scarborough
(Toronto), Ont.
TEAM: Frank Cicci

- Tracy had been expected to move to NASCAR for several years and signed with Frank Cicci to drive five Busch Series races in 2005, while continuing a full Champ Car schedule.

- He won the 2003 CART championship and became the first driver in 32 years to win the season's first three races.

- His 30 Champ Car victories are most among active drivers.

- In 1985, at the age of 16, Tracy was the youngest-ever Canadian Formula Ford Champion.

MARTIN TRUEX JR.

- In 2006 Truex became the first full-time driver of DEI's No. 1 Cup car in five years.

- He won the Busch Series championship in both 2004 and 2005.

- In 2005 he won NASCAR's first race in Mexico, the Busch Series' Telcel-Motorola 200 in Mexico City.

- He made two Nextel Cup starts for DEI in 2004 and seven in 2005. He failed to finish five races in 2005, but recorded a career-high seventh place finish at the Coca-Cola 600, after starting 30th.

NO. 1

BORN:
June 29, 1980

HOMETOWN:
Mayetta, N.J.

TEAM:
Dale Earnhardt Inc.

CAR: Chevrolet

SPONSOR: U.S. Army

SCOTT WIMMER

- Wimmer finished 32nd in the 2005 drivers' standings for Bill Davis Racing, and won $3,057,533.

- In the opening race of his first full Nextel Cup season, Wimmer finished a stunning third at the 2004 Daytona 500. He ended the season in 27th place overall.

- He won four Busch Series races and finished third in the points championship in 2002, and was runner-up to Greg Biffle for the rookie-of-the-year award.

- He was rookie of the year in 1994 in three separate series: at State Park Speedway, Dells Motor Speedway and the Wisconsin Short Track Series.

NO. 4

BORN:
January 26, 1976

HOMETOWN:
Wausau, Wis.

TEAM:
Morgan-McClure

CAR: Chevrolet

SPONSOR:
AERO Exhaust

LEGENDS

BOBBY ALLISON

BORN: December 3, 1937, Miami, Fla.

CARS DRIVEN:
Mercury, Chevrolet, Buick, AMC

YEARS IN CUP RACING:
28 (1961–1988)

CUP WINS: 85

CAREER EARNINGS:
$7,673,808

Bobby Allison had one of the most turbulent careers in NASCAR. In his 26 years of Cup racing he also had one of the most successful NASCAR careers.

Starting in 1961, until his retirement in 1998, Allison recorded 85 victories, third on the all-time win list. During those years he finished the season in the top-10 a total of 17 times, with five second-place finishes and a NASCAR championship in 1983.

His reputation as one of NASCAR's fiercest competitors started as soon as he got into the top division, when he placed 20th in Ralph Stark's Chevrolet at the 1961 Daytona 500. Even with less than optimum equipment, Allison went up against the best of drivers during

his career and, once established, drove with a presence rarely found in today's racing.

Born in Florida in December 1937, Robert Arthur Allison convinced his mother to sign for him so he could run an old coupe at Hialeah Speedway in 1955. A couple of years after that, Allison and his brother Donnie ran the NASCAR Modified races whenever they could afford to.

In 1961, with a taste for Cup racing but no money to run the series, Allison concentrated on his Modified driving, winning this division title three years in a row, from 1962 to 1964. With these credentials and a move to the more stock car–oriented atmosphere around Hueytown, Alabama, Allison managed to run eight Grand National (now Nextel Cup) races for 1965.

He ran 33 races the next year, but funds were tight. He wanted to continue, and with Donnie's help he built a Chevelle at his modest shop for the 1966 season. With this Chevelle, Allison was on his way, winning his first race at Oxford, Maine, and two more NASCAR events to finish a respectable 10th in the season.

He raced in 45 events in 1967, for Bud Moore, Cotton Owens and himself, but took two wins when he hooked up with the famed Holman-Moody team. After capturing 11 wins for Holman-Moody in 1971, Allison went to drive for Junior Johnson, picking up another 10 wins in 1972.

Over the next several years, Allison drove for several teams, including Penske and DiGard Racing. It was with the DiGard Buick and a Robert Yates engine that he won the NASCAR Winston Cup title in 1983.

Known as one of the founding members of the "Alabama Gang," Allison received national attention in 1979 during his race-ending fight with Cale Yarborough on the first live telecast of the Daytona 500. His brother Donnie had been leading the race with a lap left, and a determined Yarborough was right behind him. Entering the final turn the cars collided, ending up on the infield grass while Richard Petty cruised to the win.

While this action was taking place, Bobby Allison decided to stop and check on his brother, and after some verbal sparring, the three drivers were physically discussing their views with their fists on television.

Aside from this notoriety, or perhaps because of it, Allison was voted NASCAR's most popular driver six times. He was also bestowed NASCAR's "Award of Excellence" in 1989 and named as one of its "50 Greatest Drivers."

To show he was not just a good ol' stock car boy, he competed in SCCA Trans-Am racing and drove in two Indianapolis 500 events. He started 12th in the 1973 Indy 500, placing 32nd after throwing a rod in the early stages, and he returned in 1975, starting 15th and finishing 25th, out with a broken transmission.

Left: Bobby Allison at the Richmond 500 shows off his trophy after ending Richard Petty's seven-race winning streak. Allison won the 1974 race by beating Petty five seconds at the finish.

Opposite: Four of auto racing's top drivers duel nose to tail in the 1976 Daytona 500. From front are Bobby Allison, David Pearson, Richard Petty and A.J. Foyt.

He drove for Penske in both Indy races.

Allison also made more "star appearances" during his career than any other Cup driver, flying into oval tracks all over North America as a guest driver, and quite often winning before flying back out the same night.

In 1988 Allison was involved in a career-ending crash. Racing at Pocono, the accident left him with a broken shoulder, left leg and ribs and a brain injury. His recovery was slow but steady, and he turned his racing efforts to helping sons Clifford and Davey.

In 1992 Clifford was killed in a crash at Michigan, and Davey, a successful Cup driver for nine years, was killed in a helicopter accident at Talladega in 1993.

Along with dealing with the loss of his two sons, he lost his close friend Neil Bonnett, who was killed racing in February 1994. Allison struggled to operate his own NASCAR Cup team but called it a day in 1997.

Allison is an accomplished pilot, starting his flying in 1967. He has owned and flown a succession of Aerostar aircraft over the years. He is also a mechanical inventor of some note, developing racing engines and parts for NASCAR competition as well as aircraft engine and propeller items.

He was one of the most competitive individuals in racing. Big track, short track, road course, paved or dirt, Allison was perhaps the toughest racer to beat.

DALE EARNHARDT

BORN:
April 29, 1951,
Kannapolis, N.C.

DIED:
February 18, 2001

CAR DRIVEN:
Chevrolet

**YEARS IN CUP
RACING: 27**
(1975–2001)

CUP WINS: 76

CAREER EARNINGS:
Over $41 million

Top: Dale Earnhardt in his car at the Daytona International Speedway, hours before the tragic crash that ended his life on February 18, 2001.

With a tenacity seldom found in any professional sport, Dale Earnhardt propelled his way into the consciousness of the racing public.
Through his determination, he became a national symbol and a seven-time NASCAR Cup champion, and his name was synonymous with stock car racing.

His racing death at the end of the 2001 Daytona 500 elevated his status to an unprecedented level. To many in countries outside the United States he had represented the American dream.

Earnhardt brought more fans to NASCAR than any other driver. He was known as the "Man in Black" and the "Intimidator" for his unmatched win-at-all-costs attitude. This attitude, along with large amounts of sheer grit, thrust this Kannapolis, North Carolina, native and Grade 9 dropout not only to the top of NASCAR, but to the head of his own multi-million-dollar business. His tireless work ethic turned into the most dominant career in NASCAR history.

His racing spanned more than two decades. It included running in 676 races – and winning

76 of these. He took 281 top-five and 428 top-10 finishes. He is also the only six-time winner of the Busch Clash and the only three-time winner of the Winston All-Star race.

Earnhardt was born in 1951, and he developed a passion for stock car racing early on through his father, Ralph, a racer of some note throughout the southeastern United States. While in his teens, Earnhardt worked on his own race cars, starting with hobby-class cars, eking out a racing program that depended on winning to pay back his creditors.

When his father died in 1973, Earnhardt became more determined than ever to be a successful driver. He built cars and raced on the Sportsman circuits at such speedways as Hickory and Concord.

His first Cup ride was in the World 600 at Charlotte in 1975. He drove Ed Negre's Dodge and placed 22nd, winning $2,425. Between 1976 and 1978 he competed in eight events with limited success, but in 1979 dramatic changes were about to occur.

When Dave Marcis left car owner Rod Osterlund, the car owner put Earnhardt behind the wheel – the break Earnhardt considered the biggest in his racing career. In his first full season of Winston Cup (currently Nextel Cup) racing, he took his first victory, a win at Bristol in only his 16th Cup start. He finished the season with 11 top-five finishes, placed seventh in the standings and won rookie-of-the-year honors.

Everything came together – and quickly – in 1980, as Earnhardt won the Cup title with five wins that year. Well into the 1981 season, he drove for the well-established Bud Moore team and took a pair of races in Moore's Fords over the next two years.

Meanwhile, new team owner, Richard Childress, was starting to build a strong team, and Earnhardt got into the driver's seat starting in 1984. Little did either know what was to happen in the next few seasons.

This team effort took the driver and owner to a level of performance neither imagined, and by 1987 they had captured two Cup championships. Throughout the 1990s, the black No. 3 Chevy became a familiar sight in victory lane, and Earnhardt drove to Cup titles in 1990, 1991, 1993 and 1994. He was a force to be reckoned with and competed with a fierceness and intensity like no other on the circuit. He performed feats few thought possible, always pushing himself and his car for success.

He was often referred to as the "Master of the Draft" for his ability to use this aerodynamic force to win on superspeedways such as Talladega. Even when he developed his own racing team, Dale Earnhardt Incorporated, he continued with his nothing-ventured, nothing-gained mentality, and his status in the racing world continued to climb.

The fire that burned in him as a race car driver also burned in Earnhardt off-track. He broke new ground in the NASCAR world through marketing himself and his image. His financial successes became just as strong and positive as his racing. His attitude was endearing, and a shining example of triumph over adversity. He drove to win, no matter the circumstances.

Perhaps the best example of his persona came after he was involved in a bad crash

Top: No. 3 – the most famous image of NASCAR's modern era.

Left: A fan's tribute.

in 1996 at Talladega. He severely injured his collarbone, so much so he couldn't finish driving in the Brickyard 400 at Indy a week after his crash. It was the first time since 1979 Earnhardt could not finish a race due to an injury.

Nevertheless, two weeks after the Talladega incident, Earnhardt – in complete hard-core character, still wracked with pain – pushed himself to another level, winning pole position at the Watkins Glen road course event and placing sixth at the end of the race.

Dale Earnhardt was no quitter. That was the essence in the career of what many consider the greatest stock car driver ever.

THE FLOCKS

Tim Flock

BORN: May 11, 1924, Fort Payne, Ala.

DIED: March 31, 1998

CARS DRIVEN: Hudson, Oldsmobile, Chrysler

YEARS IN CUP RACING: 13 (1949–1961)

CUP WINS: 40

CAREER EARNINGS: $109,656

Top: The most prominent member of the Flock family, Tim Flock (left) raced Hudsons, Oldsmobiles and Chryslers. Here he is (right), congratulated after a 1957 Grand National victory, one of 40 such wins of his career. He won 18 races in 1955 alone.

In NASCAR's early years, there were a lot of charismatic drivers, but the Flock family retains a special place in the early history of the sport.

The Flock family consisted of four brothers and two sisters, and the family moved to the Atlanta area from their Alabama home for better employment opportunities during the years before World War II.

Brothers Tim, Fonty and Bob learned their driving skills hauling moonshine around the back roads of Georgia. Carl raced boats. Sister Ethel, who also made her mark in racing in those early years with over 100 races to her credit, was named after the high-test gasoline of the time. The youngest Flock, Reo, was named after the car, and she took to skydiving and wing-walking.

Born in 1924, Tim Flock started his professional racing career in 1947, running in a Modified race in North Wilkesboro, North Carolina. It was Tim who would have the most successful racing career in the family, and he was on his way when he placed fifth at Charlotte in 1949 in NASCAR's new "Strictly Stock" division, a forerunner of today's Nextel Cup.

He was driving an Olds 88, one of the hottest cars at the time. Older brother Fonty took second in the race, driving one of the "Step-Down" Hudsons. The following year, Tim won his first NASCAR race, winning the Grand National event at Charlotte.

For the next several years, Tim Flock became a dominant force in Grand National racing. He won his first championship in 1952 behind the wheel of Ted Chester's Hudson, taking eight NASCAR events and finishing 14 times in the top five.

After an altercation with NASCAR in 1954 over some engine modifications, resulting in then-president Bill France taking away his victory, Bill Flock said he would not race NASCAR again. So he opened up a Pure Oil station in Atlanta and seemed content with his new life. Then in 1955, friends convinced him to travel to Daytona. Remarking out loud he could win the Daytona race if he had one of the new Chrysler 300s tearing down the sand during the beach trials, Flock found himself introduced to Carl Kiekhaefer, the man behind the Chrysler assault on NASCAR.

The Mercury Outboard Motor president

needed another driver for his team. Flock got into one of the big Hemi-powered Chryslers and took the pole for the Daytona Beach race. He placed second in the race behind Fireball Roberts, but Roberts' car was deemed illegal, so Flock was on his way. In 1955 he won 18 of his 40 Grand National races and his second NASCAR championship. His 1955 winning season was a NASCAR record that was not broken until Richard Petty won 19 races in 1967.

Tim Flock ran with Kiekhaefer and the Chryslers in 1956, with three wins in his first eight races. However, the spirited Flock was tired of the strict regimentation of Kiekhaefer and quit the team.

He continued to race but never with the same amount of success. In 1961 he ran afoul of Bill France when he attempted to organize a drivers' union with fellow driver Curtis Turner, and both drivers were banned from NASCAR.

Although the ban was lifted in 1966, Tim had soured on driving. He did stay in racing, though, working as program director at the Charlotte Motor Speedway.

Inducted into the International Motorsports Press Hall of Fame in 1991 and the Stock Car Hall of Fame in 1995, Tim Flock died in 1998. He had won 40 races and 37 pole positions in his 13-year NASCAR career. With the 40 victories in 189 starts, Tim Flock holds a winning percentage of 21.2, the best in NASCAR Grand National/Cup history. He also won NASCAR's only sports car race, in 1955, driving a Mercedes-Benz 300SL Gullwing.

Older brother Fonty did not have as successful a career as Tim, but he was a force to reckon with in NASCAR's early days. Running in semi-organized events prior to World War II, Fonty did well, but he was severely injured in a crash at Daytona in 1941 and didn't return to racing until 1947.

In May of that year, he won the inaugural stock car race at North Wilkesboro, and continued with victories at Charlotte, Trenton and Greensboro, winning the National Championship Stock Car Circuit, the name used before NASCAR.

In 1949, Fonty won NASCAR's Modified title with 11 victories, and then took to Grand National racing, finishing second in 1951, fourth in 1952 and fifth in 1953. He drove a limited schedule starting in 1954, and after a crash at Darlington in 1957, he parked it for good.

Sister Ethel was not just a flash in the pan racer. Driving brother Fonty's Modified in the late 1940s, she raced in more than 100 events. Although she usually limited her racing to the Atlanta area, she did make a trip to Daytona in July 1949 and drove her Cadillac to an 11th-place finish in a field of 26 competitors, ahead of brothers Fonty and Bob. She also finished ahead of such early notables as Herb Thomas, Curtis Turner and Buck Baker.

Tim's older brother Fonty shown at Daytona with one of the Chrysler 300s of 1955–56. NASCAR's 1949 Modified champ, Fonty stopped racing in 1957.

DAVID PEARSON

BORN:
December 22, 1934,
Whitney, S.C.

CARS DRIVEN:
Dodge, Ford,
Mercury

**YEARS IN CUP
RACING:** 27
(1960–1986)

CUP WINS: 105

CAREER EARNINGS:
$2,836,224

Top: Pearson, the
Wood Brothers and
the Mercury after the
Firecracker win at
Daytona in 1976.

One of the great stock car drivers, David Pearson amassed 105 NASCAR Cup victories, second only to all-time leader Richard Petty with 200 wins.

There were times during his 27-year career where his star shone bright. Many speculate that if Pearson had raced as long as Petty he would have taken the title as the "King of Stock Car Racing."

This South Carolina native, born in 1934, was NASCAR champ three times and leads the all-time win ration with 18 percent. As a sample of his strength, Pearson entered only 18 races in 1973 but won 11 of these events.

Pearson started his racing career in 1952 on the dirt tracks near his home. By 1960 he was on the NASCAR circuit, and he took 18th at Daytona that year. The next year he won his first Grand National race (the forerunner of today's Nextel Cup), the World 600, plus the Firecracker 250 and the Dixie 400 at Atlanta, and was the first driver to accomplish this in a single year. He won the 1961 rookie-of-the-year honors with his Chevy, and his reputation was on its way.

Throughout the 1960s, Pearson was a dominant racer in NASCAR's top class, first running in Dodges and then switching over to the familiar No. 21 Mercury and Ford Talladega mounts.

Pearson's physical attributes played a large part in his success. He was stout in stature, and those days it took a lot of muscle to handle a car in a long race when there was no power steering.

In 1964 he won eight events on the short tracks, and two years later won 10 of 15 races on dirt tracks and enough events on the remainder of the circuit to give him his first NASCAR championship.

By the end of the decade, Pearson's late-race hold-nothing-back, pedal-to-the-floor style had taken hold, and in both 1968 and 1969 he won top honors again.

In 1968, he drove his Ford to 16 wins, and in 1969, he took 11 wins. In those two years he also led 37 and 39 races, respectively. He was the first to break the 190 mile-per-hour barrier at Daytona, qualifying his Ford at 190.029 miles per hour in 1969.

Pearson acquired the nickname "The Silver Fox" for his driving prowess. He was a master at playing his cards close to the vest, never showing what he was capable of until the closing laps of a race. When he was running well, he would lurk back a few positions from the leader, and then near the end would turn it up a few notches to get in the lead on the last lap.

During this heady time in NASCAR history, the rivalry between Pearson and Petty elevated the sport's awareness. Their late-race duels became a mainstay at many a track, and were always exciting, offering some of the most memorable finishes in NASCAR racing. This duo finished one-two 63 times, Pearson taking 33 victories and Petty 30.

One of this pair's most famous finishes occurred at the end of the 1976 Daytona 500, a race Pearson had never won in 17 attempts. As Pearson and Petty entered the last lap on the 2.5-mile oval, Petty led, and all waited for Pearson to make his move. Going into turn three Pearson took the lead, but drifted high near the wall in doing so, and Petty regained the lead, but by only a couple of feet. The two tangled in turn four, with Pearson going into the wall and

Petty sliding down into the infield. The "King" was 50 yards away from winning – 50 yards away from the start/finish line with a car he couldn't get started.

With no other cars on the lead lap, Pearson managed to keep the engine running in his Mercury, collected the battered car back up, and limped across the line to win his first Daytona 500.

Pearson did win races after his Daytona victory, but the glory days were gone. He had a couple of wins in 1979 and 1980, winning his last Cup event at Darlington, a treacherous track he was able to master.

Although he never suffered any race-related injuries during his career, Pearson's eyesight was not as good as it once was and, troubled with persistent back problems as well, he retired from driving in 1986 at age 52.

In 1967, race cars had big engines and real bumpers. That's David Pearson (No. 17) and Mario Andretti (No. 11) sliding in unison while Petty tries to sneak by on the high side during the National 500 at Charlotte.

Left: David Pearson, with the 1976 Southern 500 trophy.

RICHARD PETTY

BORN: July 2, 1937, Level Cross, N.C.

CARS DRIVEN: Plymouth, Pontiac

YEARS IN CUP RACING: 35 (1958–1992)

CUP WINS: 200

CAREER EARNINGS: $8,541,218

Richard Petty buckles his safety belt as he prepares for practice rounds for the 1972 Pennsylvania 500.

When one thinks of stock car racing, one cannot help but think of Richard Petty. To many fans, he is stock car racing.

During his 35-year racing career, this lanky, dark-haired North Carolina native epitomized stock car racing, and became not only the sport's most famous figure, but one of the most famous personalities in all sports. His status with his fans is akin to Elvis Presley, and Petty has truly become the "King" of his sport.

Over his three decades of racing, Petty has deservedly earned his crown, both on and off the track. Not only did he amass a track record that may never be equaled, he did it in his characteristic humble style. With his trademark cowboy boots and hat, Petty always took time at races to sign autographs and chat with people. He always said if it wasn't for the fans, he would not have had such a long and illustrious career.

Nevertheless, his driving skills played an important role in his racing, from the dirt bullrings in his early years to the superspeedways before he hung up his hat. He was a major part of NASCAR's growth and traditions as it established itself from a small regional series to a major nationally conscious sport. Just some of his accomplishments include:

• Most Cup wins, with 200
• Most laps led, with 52,194
• Most races led, with 599
• Most consecutive races won, with 10 in 1967
• Most wins in one season, with 27 in 1967

Born in Level Cross, North Carolina, in July 1937, Petty grew up in a racing environment. His father, Lee Petty, was one of the stars during NASCAR's first decade, twice winning the Grand National (today's equivalent of the Nextel Cup) title, and winning the first Daytona 500 in 1959.

The Pettys were family-oriented, and all members not only went to the races as a group, they helped with the operation. Richard and brother Maurice crewed for their father, and Mother Elizabeth scored for the team.

Soon it was Richard's turn to race a car.

"My daddy was a race driver, so I became a race driver," Petty said. "If he'd been a grocer, I might have been a grocer. If he'd been a baseball player, I'd probably have wanted to be a baseball player. But he was a race driver, so here I am."

Just after his 21st birthday, Petty entered his first NASCAR race, driving an Oldsmobile in NASCAR's Convertible Class. He finished sixth in that 200-lapper on the old Columbia, South Carolina, dirt oval. His first win came a year later, in 1959, at the same track.

In 1960, Petty won his first Grand National race, and two years later he finished second in points in NASCAR's top division. In 1963, he captured 14 wins, then in 1964 he won his first of seven Daytona 500 races and also won the division championship.

He then left NASCAR to drag race – yes, drag race – just as his stock car career was taking off.

By 1964 auto manufacturers were producing the most powerful engines in racing history, and NASCAR teams picked up on this trend with Ford's 427-cubic-inch engine and Chrysler's 426-cubic-inch Hemi-head engine. However, with no end in sight for this horse-power race, NASCAR outlawed these "power plants." So at the request of Petty's sponsor, Chrysler, the blue No. 43 Plymouth was parked for most of the 1965 season, and the team went drag racing.

Petty campaigned an altered-wheel-base Plymouth Barracuda, a forerunner of today's Funny Car. While touring the southern United States, Petty and his team learned NASCAR had modified the engine restrictions for its premier class. He returned to his stock car roots, winning four races before the end of the season.

By 1967 Petty was becoming an icon in stock car racing, and by 1971 had won his third Daytona 500 as well as his third Grand National championship. In 1972 the now-famous No. 43 was sponsored by STP. By 1980 Petty added four more driving titles to his resume, capturing the top spot in 1972, 1974, 1975 and 1979. In 1981 he won the Daytona 500 for the seventh time.

Then, in 1982, the Petty team switched from their long association with Chrysler products to General Motors' Pontiac division, and Richard's son Kyle joined the team as a driver – the third generation of Pettys to compete in NASCAR. Richard's last two victories were the Daytona Pepsi Firecracker 400 and the Dover Budweiser 500, both in 1984.

At the end of the 1992 season, at 55 years of age, Richard Petty retired from competitive driving. During his final year, he was honored at each race by the fans and his fellow drivers.

He was also honored with the highest civilian award in the United States, the Medal of Freedom. Since then, Petty has been inducted into several auto racing and sports halls of fame, and has received numerous press awards. Still, Petty's greatest personal achievement has been the adoration of his fans. He won the Most Popular NASCAR Driver Award nine times, and to most race fans he will always be the "King."

Petty in the STP car during the 1994 Daytona 500.

Left: Richard Petty sprays champagne in the victory circle at the Daytona International Speedway after winning the 1984 Firecracker 400 – his 200th career win.

GLENN "FIREBALL" ROBERTS

BORN:
January 20, 1929,
Daytona Beach,
Florida

DIED:
July 2, 1964

CARS DRIVEN:
Pontiac, Ford,
Chevrolet

YEARS IN CUP: 16
(1949–1964)

WINS: 33

EARNINGS: $305,960

Roberts in one of the dominant Smokey Yunick-prepared Pontiacs, here at Daytona in 1959. Compare his racing attire with that of today's drivers.

A master of the superspeedways, Edward Glenn "Fireball" Roberts has been called one of NASCAR's greatest drivers, and his persona dominated stock car racing in the late 1950s and early 1960s. He was a superstar before the named had been coined. While his star did not burn long, it burned brighter than that of any other driver.

Watching Roberts driving those big Pontiacs around the superspeedway in the early 1960s is one of NASCAR's greatest images. If it wasn't for his untimely death in 1964, Roberts would have surely ranked as one of the sport's greatest.

After a so-so racing career starting with NASCAR in 1949, Roberts entered his element on the new, fast, paved speedways, starting with the Firecracker 250 at Daytona in 1959. In 1962 he won both the Firecracker and Daytona 500 races on the big Daytona track, and his nickname suited his driving on the big tracks. He was calculating, crafty and knowledgeable, and was the best at the "sling shot" pass, now part of "drafting."

Born in Daytona Beach, Florida, in 1931, Roberts got his nickname for his pitching abil-

ity in high-school baseball, and although he attended the University of Florida for a while, his heart was telling him to go racing.

Placing second in NASCAR points in 1950, Roberts divided his racing between the Grand National and Modified divisions, and in 1956 won five GN events.

But in 1959 a new era of stock car racing began with the opening of the superspeedways – tracks such as Charlotte and Daytona, paved ovals of two miles or more in length, where drivers could attain new benchmarks of speed.

Also in 1959 Roberts began his relationship with legendary race car builder Henry "Smokey" Yunick, and this combination was a tough one to beat for the next several years as Roberts' racing career took off driving those black and gold Pontiacs of Yunick.

Running 30 superspeedway races from 1959 to 1962, Roberts won five of them, and put the Pontiac on the pole in 15. His favorite playground was Daytona, where he won so often that fans started calling the track "Fireball International Raceway."

By the time Roberts was 30 years old, the

sport was starting to wear on him. His passion was not what it once was, and he was not as dominant. By 1964 he would spin out on tracks that he had previously mastered. He admitted to friends he wanted out, maybe try his hand at broadcasting. He also mentioned getting out entirely and buying a beer distributorship.

But he was contractually bound to race for the Ford team of Holman-Moody and the sponsors. In May 1964 he headed to Charlotte and the World 600, which would be his last race.

Prophetically, Fireball's car hit the wall and burst into flames after getting into a smash-up with Junior Johnson and Ned Jarrett. With the help of Jarrett, Roberts was able to get out of the burning Ford, but he suffered burns to 75 percent of his body. He held on in hospital, but died six weeks later at the age of 35.

During his career, Roberts won 32 Grand National races, including four victories at Daytona. He set more than 400 NASCAR records. He was inducted into the International Motorsports Hall of Fame in 1990 and the Stock Car Hall Fame in 1993.

Fireball Roberts holding a trophy, around 1960. During his racing career he set more than 400 records.

Top: With the front wheels of his Ford cranked over, Roberts gets sideways in the Yankee 300.

MARSHALL TEAGUE

BORN:
February 17, 1922,
Daytona Beach,
Florida

DIED:
February 11, 1959

CARS DRIVEN:
Hudson

**YEARS IN CUP
RACING:** 4

WINS: 7

EARNINGS: $10,060

Marshall Teague
tightens his helmet
as he settles himself
in the cockpit of
his car at Daytona,
February 10, 1959.
The following day
Teague was killed
when his car crashed
after it went into a
slide on the west turn
of the track.

Marshall Teague was one of NASCAR's pioneer drivers and one of the first in the new sport to realize the importance of promotion.

Born in 1922, this Daytona Beach garage owner won seven races from 1951 to 1953, driving his famed Hudson Hornet. Teague realized the potential of the Hudson of that era, which featured superior handling characteristics over the Oldsmobiles and Plymouths. He went to the Hudson factory in Detroit and was the first driver to acquire factory support from the car maker, which supplied him with "export" options, such as heavy-duty suspension and engine parts.

Known as the "King of the Beach" for his victories on the early Daytona beach-road course, Teague took second to Robert "Red" Byron in the first-ever NASCAR-sanctioned race, a modified event held on the Daytona course in February 1948. He won five Grand National races in the 1951 season in only 15 starts.

Teague set his sights farther west in 1953 and began racing in the stock car ranks of the American Automobile Association and the U.S. Auto Club circuits. NASCAR founder Bill France did not appreciate Teague racing for rival sanctioning bodies, so Teague left NASCAR.

His AAA and USAC career was somewhat disappointing over the next few years. But Teague returned to his NASCAR roots in 1959. And it wasn't to race stock cars.

In 1959 a new era of stock car racing began with the opening of the superspeedways. These new tracks were paved ovals of two miles or more in length, where drivers could attain new benchmarks of speed. France had just finished building Daytona, the first of the superspeedways. To promote this new paved facility, he posted a $10,000 prize for the first driver to attain 160 miles per hour.

Driving a special, home-built, open-wheeled Indy-style car, Teague took to the new tri-oval on February 11, 1959. But aerodynamics and wind-tunnel testing were not part of auto racing yet, and Teague's car got out of control, flipped over, and killed him. He was 36.

CURTIS TURNER

Curtis Turner was the poster boy of stock car racing in the early years. This hard-driving, hard-working and hard-drinking Virginian lived his life the way he wanted and was the most colorful personality to get on a racetrack in the 1950s and 1960s.

Turner was a master when behind the wheel. He was hard on his cars and not averse to running others off the track to win a race – his nickname was "Pops," as he would "pop" slower cars out of his way.

Born in the Blue Ridge Mountains of Virginia in 1924, Turner won his first race in 1949. The victory was his first of over 350 wins, including 18 NASCAR Grand National wins and 38 NASCAR Convertible division victories.

Turner is the only driver to win two Grand National races in a row from the pole by leading every lap, which happened on tracks in Rochester, New York, and Charlotte, North Carolina, in 1950. He is the only one to win 25 major NASCAR events in one season driving the same car.

Later in his racing career, Turner was the first to qualify for a Grand National race at a speed greater than 180 miles per hour, which

he accomplished at the 1967 Daytona 500.

Turner was the man behind the construction of the Charlotte Motor Speedway. The concept, financing and construction were his, but when it opened in 1960, there were serious money problems. Turner did everything possible to get the track's financing in order, but he was out of his league and the track's board of directors ousted him as president in 1961.

Later that year, Turner tried to organize NASCAR drivers as a union entity. NASCAR President Bill France put a stop to that and gave Turner a lifetime suspension.

France and Turner made up in 1965, and Turner returned to plying his trade in Grand National events, but his presence at the tracks dwindled. NASCAR was becoming a professional sport with a national presence, and there was no room in it for the on-and-off track antics that made Turner famous.

Turner was an accomplished pilot. He frequently flew on business matters without incident, but then in October 1970, while flying with golfer Clarence King, Turner's plane crashed in Pennsylvania with no survivors. He was 46.

BORN: April 12, 1924, Floyd, Va.

DIED: October 14, 1970

CARS DRIVEN: Oldsmobile, Ford

YEARS IN CUP RACING: 20 (1949–1968)

CUP WINS: 17

CAREER EARNINGS: $122,155

Charismatic is a mild term for Curtis Turner, one of NASCAR's best drivers in the early years. He could drive anything and win. He was the first to qualify for a Cup race at over 180 mph, running Smokey Yunick's controversial Chevelle at Daytona in 1967.

RUSTY WALLACE

BORN: August 14, 1956, St. Louis, Mo.

CARS DRIVEN: Dodge

YEARS IN CUP RACING: 26 (1980–2005)

CUP WINS: 55

CAREER EARNINGS: $48,539,476

Rusty Wallace's racing career spanned over a quarter of a century. His legacy includes 10 straight years among the elite 10 in points standing – and a Cup win at Martinsville just a year before he retired.

For a short while, it looked as if "Rusty's Last Call" might be the roar of a championship celebration.

NASCAR is full of such over-the-top stories that when Rusty Wallace, still sailing along at the age of 59, finished third in his final race at Dover International Speedway, there was a sense that he might just accomplish the impossible, and the immortal: win a Nextel Cup championship in his final year of racing.

With that top-five at Dover, Wallace moved into second place in the Nextel Cup points standings – with eight races still remaining in the 2005 Chase. Since he'd already announced his retirement and was promoting the season as "Rusty's Last Call," contending so late in the game caught the public's attention.

Wallace eventually finished in eighth overall, and stepped out of the familiar Penske No. 2 Dodge with his head held high, a fierce competitor to the very end. He did not win a race in his 25th and final year of Cup driving, and won only once in the final 107 races of his Cup career, but he did nail down 17 top-10 finishes, tying his highest total in five years.

The charismatic Wallace left Cup racing with 706 starts, the 1989 Nextel Cup Series Championship, the eighth-highest win total in history (55) and a stunning top-10 total of 349. That translates to a top-10 finish nearly every second start. He fell just 28 laps short of completing 20,000 in his career.

In a year when many drivers complained about tires, Wallace's experience helped him to steady finishes and he completed his final season without a single DNF. It was the first time in his career he'd done that and he was the only driver among the top 30 in 2005 who wasn't forced out all season.

Wallace is from Missouri, the "Show Me" state, and that's exactly what he'll be doing in his next career. He'll show racing fans the state of the game. He was hired by ABC/ESPN to become the network's lead analyst for auto racing.

"I love talking about the sport and I love educating people about the sport," Wallace said.

Wallace's on-track legacy includes 10 straight years among the elite 10 in the points standing, a streak that ended when he finished 14th in 2004. When he finished 16th the next year, it appeared that his run near the top was done.

But then he returned with that farewell season.

When Wallace did not record a victory in 2002, it ended a 16-season stretch in which he recorded at least one Cup victory. That stands behind only Richard Petty (28) and David Pearson (17).

He didn't win again until Martinsville, the eighth race of 2004, which proved to be the final victory of his magnificent career.

"It's an honor to be compared to those guys, such as Petty, Allison or Pearson," Wallace said. "I questioned a lot of things during that dry spell."

The oldest of three brothers who would all graduate to Cup driving, Wallace is the son of Russ Wallace, who won three track championships in St. Louis. Rusty and siblings Mike and Kenny gravitated to the sport early. Wallace was the Central Racing Association's rookie of the year in 1973, and over the next five years won more than 200 stock car races before joining the USAC circuit in 1979. It was a fabulous debut year, as he won five races and was second in the points standings.

Roger Penske gave him a couple of Winston Cup rides in 1980, and Wallace made the most of the opportunity, finishing second to the late Dale Earnhardt in his debut in Atlanta. He got into seven more Cup races over the next two years, took 1983 off to win the ASA championship, and joined NASCAR Cup racing full-time in 1984, driving for Cliff Stewart. He finished 14th as a rookie, starting a string of 22 seasons among the top 20.

He joined Raymond Beadle in 1986 and won his first race, at Bristol, which he calls his favorite track. He moved up to sixth in the points standing, then fifth in 1987. When he won six times in 1988, and was runner-up to series champion Bill Elliott by just 24 points, NASCAR observers knew they were watching a future Cup champion.

The future arrived only a year later, when Wallace again won six races and edged Earnhardt by 12 points for the 1989 Winston Cup championship.

In 1991 Wallace jumped to Penske as driver and co-owner of the Miller Genuine Draft Pontiac, which would become a familiar sight among race leaders. He did have a down year in 1992, winning just once and finishing 13th overall.

But he rebounded spectacularly in 1993, with a career-high 10 victories, 21 top-10 placings and his second runner-up finish to Dale Earnhardt in the points championship. He also led the most laps that year.

Over the next nine years he finished third, fifth, fourth, eighth, ninth and seventh (four times), before dropping out to 14th in 2001. When he didn't win again the next two years, it looked as if the final victory of his career might have been the 2001 triumph at California.

But he won that 2004 race at Martinsville, then came back with a fabulous farewell fanfare in 2005. Then he walked away from his car, into the broadcast booth and into the Hall of Fame.

Wallace is acknowledged by fans after a ceremony before his last race, August 27, 2005, at the Bristol Motor Speedway.

DARRELL WALTRIP

BORN:
February 5, 1947, Owensboro, Ky.

CAR DRIVEN:
Chevrolet

YEARS IN CUP RACING: 29
(1972–2000)

CUP WINS: 84

CAREER EARNINGS:
Over $19 million

Darrell Waltrip driving his Tide No. 17 car during the Daytona 500, 1989. After 17 years of trying, he won the big race.

One of NASCAR's most emotional moments was the Victory Lane celebration at the 1989 Daytona 500.
After 17 years of trying, Darrell Waltrip won the big race.

Born in Kentucky in February 1947, Waltrip entered NASCAR's top level in 1972 at the Winston 500. He was colorful and controversial in his early Cup years, never hesitating to speak his mind – much to the disdain of the racing establishment.

Then this brash, bold youngster from Franklin, Tennessee, started to put up rather than shut up. He won his first race at the 1975 running of the Music City 420 in Nashville, and by 1981 had picked up his first of three NASCAR Winston Cup championships.

To keep silencing his critics, he also won the title in 1982, with another 12 race victories. He won his third title in 1985.

By now Waltrip's former nickname of "Jaws" had been replaced by "Ol' D.W.," as he had definitely earned the respect of both drivers and fans by driving for legendary car owner Junior Johnson.

Waltrip started racing on dirt with a 1936

Chevy coupe after a stint at karting. But the 16-year-old didn't take to the dirt tracks, so he focused on pavement ovals, where he became an ace in short-track competition.

When Waltrip moved to the Nashville area, he made a name in local Late Model Sportsman racing. He also ran a lot of American Speed Association (ASA) races in the early 1970s with this Midwest-based group.

In October 1972, an ASA race at Salem, Indiana, gave the world a taste of what to expect from Waltrip. After a week's rain delay, Waltrip returned to the track and was leading one of the two 100-lap qualifiers for the main event when his transmission locked up, putting him out of the race.

He was given a ride in another driver's car for the final, starting last in a 30-car field featuring the best in short-track racing. So not only was Ol' D.W. starting from scratch, but it was getting dark in Salem. There were no track lights, and race organizers figured there was no way to complete 100 laps.

"We had a quick drivers' meeting before lining up the final," recalled race promoter Steve Stubbs. "When we think it's getting too dark, we'll put out a '10-to-go' sign, regardless of how many laps are completed to that point.

"Thence proceeds one of the damndest driving exhibitions I've ever seen and I've seen a few. D.W. passed cars up against the fence, then down in the dirt, then between 'em, you name it. He was coming like death and taxes.

"With 38 laps in, John Potts (the flagman) hangs out the '10-to-go' sign and D.W. is now about fifth. Larry Moore, the hotdog of that era, was leading. Six laps later D.W. catches him, they battle tooth 'n' nail, he goes by with two to go and wins it by two car lengths!

"The last few laps, the only way you could tell where the cars were is by the blue flame coming out the exhausts. It was a wild and woolly affair, for sure."

Waltrip made his living racing the bullrings, and he was good at it. With some family help, he made a few forays into NASCAR in the early 1970s, and by 1975 felt he was ready to step up to NASCAR's top class. However, he knew the step would be difficult and challenging.

"Wherever I would go, I was almost assured I was going to win one or two races a week and I made a good living doing that," Waltrip said about his short-track career. "It was hard to step up to the big leagues and be just another fish in a big pond. So it took some time to make up my mind that I needed to get in there, give it 100 percent, and make my mark."

Waltrip indeed made his mark. Not only did he win the three Cup titles, he was runner-up in 1979, 1983 and 1986. His victory total of 84 earned him a third-place tie with Bobby Allison on the all-time NASCAR most-wins list, and with 59 career Cup poles, he is fourth on that all-time NASCAR list.

Waltrip is also the only five-time winner of the World 600 at Charlotte, and he won the inaugural Winston All-Star race in 1985 at Charlotte. He was the first Cup driver to earn $10 million, which occurred in 1990.

Waltrip's last win came in 1992 in the Southern 500 at Darlington, and he finished ninth in the standings. He continued to race and was still competitive, but by 1996 was 29th in the

standings. In 2000, his last year of Cup racing, he finished 36th.

He stayed with racing, though, driving in a few NASCAR Craftsman Truck Series events, which led him to field a team in this division. At present he heads up a team in this series with a Toyota truck and driver David Reutimann.

Waltrip has put his vocal powers to good use these past few seasons with the Fox Television Network as a commentator and race analyst for its Nextel Cup presentations. Aside from these duties, Waltrip owns a Honda dealership in his hometown of Franklin, and his recent autobiography made the *New York Times* bestseller list.

Darrell Waltrip backed up his early brashness with a successful NASCAR career.

HENRY "SMOKEY" YUNICK

BORN:
May 25, 1923, Tenn.

DIED: May 9, 2001

CARS: Hudson, Chevrolet, Ford, Pontiac

YEARS IN CUP RACING: On and off from 1956 to 1969

WINS: 9

EARNINGS: $109,665

Smokey Yunick inspects the underside of one of his Indy Champ race cars. A pair of chrome-plated hands warns the curious to keep off.

In a sport filled with colorful characters in its early years, none was as colorful as Henry "Smokey" Yunick.

Not only was Smokey Yunick a master mechanic who fielded a massive quantity of race cars for several decades, he brought his technological improvements to the auto racing world. His reputation as a mechanical genius continues to this day.

From his shop in Daytona Beach, called "The Best Damn Garage in Town," Yunick was one of the most innovative men in racing in the United States, and the most famous and influential crew chief/mechanic in NASCAR history. Yunick's cars won over 50 races, and his association with more than 50 drivers includes some of the most prominent in U.S. racing.

Yunick's most legendary achievement was his ability to circumvent standard racing rules and technology. He didn't bend the rules, but he massaged them. He not only thought outside the box; his creative juices worked at a whole other level from those of his contemporaries.

Born in 1923, Yunick was raised on a Pennsylvania farm, and working on tractors started

his mechanical creativity. While running in a motorcycle race in 1941, the announcer forgot his name. Yunick's bike was smoking a lot on the track, so he acquired the nickname "Smokey."

Signing up for World War II, Yunick saw action in several theaters, mostly piloting a B-17 bomber, but he also flew with the Flying Tigers in Asia, and flew supplies over the "Hump" to China.

Not liking cold weather, Yunick set up shop in Daytona Beach in 1946, and started his long career building Hudson Hornet engines for NASCAR pioneer driver Herb Thomas. In the mid-50s he applied his genius to Chevrolet and then Ford, switching over to Pontiac with drivers Fireball Roberts, Paul Goldsmith and Marvin Panch. His cars won four of the first eight major races at Daytona through to 1962.

He continued to field stock cars from 1963 to 1968, with drivers such as Banjo Matthews, Bobby Issac and Curtis Turner.

Yunick also spent a lot of time at Indianapolis, applying his talents to the speedy Champ cars. After learning about the oval cars that had no fenders, Yunick built several cars from

1958 to 1975. He never achieved the success of his stock car efforts, although he did win at the Brickyard in 1960 with driver Jim Rathman.

On the NASCAR scene, Yunick switched back to Chevrolet in 1963, and helped develop the new big-block 427-cubic-inch engine for the GM division. Although Chevy was officially out of NASCAR racing, Yunick continued to work with Chevy in a semi-secret fashion, fielding a series of Chevelle-based cars as an independent.

During this time NASCAR, prodded by the factory-based Chrysler and Ford teams, paid close attention to Yunick's winning cars – with a lot of fighting over rules interpretation going on between Yunick and the NASCAR tech inspectors.

The most famous incident occurred in 1968 at Daytona, when NASCAR officials found 16 rules infractions in the Chevelle race car – after it had gone through tech inspection – including a reference to fuel hidden somewhere in the car other than the gas tank.

Legend has it that after this flawed inspection, Yunick got in the car and drove it back to his Daytona Beach garage.

The Chevelle's fuel tank was sitting back at the track's inspection area.

He left the NASCAR arena in 1970, worked on Indy cars for a few years, but then quit racing altogether to continue his work on inventing and conservation issues.

It was during this time that he started to travel to the oil fields of Ecuador to work with the oil companies, making the oil-producing machinery function better using the more environmentally friendly hydrogen and natural gas.

He also retained an interest in aviation, and flew helicopters for about 30 years. In 1947 he started a truck dealership in Daytona Beach and remained a dealer until the late 1980s. He was a technical adviser and personal consultant to many automobile, automobile-related and oil companies. He wrote several books and was on the staff of a number of auto magazines for 30 years. His inventions, some of which are in the Smithsonian Institution, include variable ratio power steering, extended tip spark plugs, race track crash barriers and hot vapor engines.

The list of Yunick's drivers reads like a who's who in U.S. racing. Some of the NASCAR drivers include Bobby Allison, Paul Goldsmith, Tim and Fonty Flock, Curtis Turner, Fireball Roberts, Ralph Moody, Buck Baker and Cotton Owens. Indy car drivers include Al and Bobby Unser, Mario Andretti, A.J. Foyt, Joe Leonard, Gordon Johncock and Tony Bettenhausen. Other notables include David Hobbs, Jim Hall and Mickey Thompson.

Smokey Yunick won 57 Cup races, and one Indianapolis 500 (in 1960). He has been inducted into the National Racing Hall of Fame, the International Motorsports Hall of Fame and the Stock Car Racing Hall of Fame at Daytona.

He died in May 2001.

Yunick gives a guided tour of the Daytona track to the chairman of the board of the Goodyear Tire and Rubber Co., May 1964.

GLOSSARY

Aerodynamics The science of understanding different forces acting on a moving element in gases such as air. As applied to racing, the study of airflow and the forces of resistance and pressure that result from the flow of air over, under and around a moving car. The application of this study to racing is credited with much of the sport's recent progress as teams learn more about drag, air turbulence and downforce.

Air dam The front valance of the vehicle, which produces downforce while directing air flow around the car.

Anti-roll bars Bars running in the front of the car, which help control how much the car tips from side to side; linking suspension parts which can be adjusted to alter handling characteristics to compensate for tire wear and varying fuel loads.

Apron The paved portion of a racetrack which separates the racing surface from the (usually unpaved) infield. The very bottom of the racetrack, below the bottom groove. If a car has a problem, the driver goes there to get out of the way.

Back stretch The straight on a circle track between turns two and three.

Backup car A secondary complete and set-up stock car brought to NASCAR races by each team, transported and stored in the front half of the upper level of team haulers. Backup cars must pass all NASCAR inspections. The backup car may not be unloaded at any time during all NASCAR National Series practice or pre-race competition activities unless the primary car is damaged beyond repair.

Balance A term that aero engineers use to describe downforce, front to rear. Balance is also used to explain the situation when, in a perfect world, the least amount of drag is produced for the most downforce exerted.

Banking The sloping of a racetrack, particularly at a curve or corner, from the apron to the outside wall. "Degree of banking" refers to the height of a track's slope at its outside edge.

Black box Unlike airplane black boxes, which store recording devices, a race car's black box contains high-tech electrical systems that control most engine functions. More technically referred to as the "engine electronic controls," the "engine control unit" or the "engine management system."

Blister Excessive heat can make a tire literally blister and shed rubber. Drivers can detect the problem by the resulting vibrations, and risk more serious damage if they choose not to pit.

Blocking Changing position on the track to prevent drivers behind from passing. Blocking is accepted if a car is defending position in the running order, but considered unsportsmanlike if lapped cars hold up more competitive teams.

Brake scoop Openings in the body panel and other locations of a stock car which take in air for cooling. A maximum of three scoops per brake is permitted by NASCAR officials, with a maximum of three-inch flexible hose to the brake.

Bump drafting A version of drafting in which one car bumps another. The initial contact breaks downforce and drag forces momentarily, giving the lead car as much as 100 more usable horsepower, rocketing it away from the pack without totally breaking the draft.

Camber The angle that wheels are tilted inward or outward (the angle that a tire seizes to the track surface) from vertical. If the top of the wheel is tilted inward, the camber is negative.

Caster The angle of a spindle frontward or rearward. "Caster stagger" is the difference between the static caster settings; it affects the amount of pull to the right or left a driver experiences. The more caster stagger, the more the vehicle pulls or steers.

Chassis The basic structure of a race car to which all other components are attached. CART cars have carbon-fiber monocoque tubes, while a NASCAR stock car has a steel tube frame chassis.

Chute A racetrack straightaway, either on an oval or a road course.

Circulating Driving around a track with a damaged and/or slow car to accumulate laps and, more importantly, points and prize money.

Combinations Combinations of engine, gearing, suspension, aerodynamic parts, and wheel and tire settings which teams forecast will work under varying conditions and tracks. These combinations (also known as set-ups) are recorded and used as baseline when teams arrive at a track.

Compound The rubber blend for tires. In some series, teams can choose their tire compound based on the track and weather conditions. A softer compound tire provides better traction but wears out much faster than a harder compound tire, which doesn't provide as much grip. Different tracks require different tire compounds. Left-side tires are considerably softer than right-side tires and it's against the rules to run left sides on the right.

Dialed in A car that is handling very well. The car isn't loose or tight; it's comfortable to the driver's liking.

Dirty air Turbulent air caused by fast-moving cars, which can cause a particular car to lose control. "I got in his air."

DNF Did not finish.

DNQ Did not qualify.

DNS Did not start.

Downforce The downward pressure of the air on a car as it races. Downforce increases with velocity, or the rapidity of motion or speed. It is determined by such things as front fenders and rear spoilers.

Draft Airflow creates a low-pressure air pocket (or draft) behind moving objects. Most notably in NASCAR, drivers try to follow opponents closely enough to enter their draft and benefit from a towing effect. The car creating the draft actually pulls the pursuing driver, who can ease off the throttle and save gas.

Drafting Practice of two or more cars to run nose to tail while racing, almost touching. The lead car, by displacing air in front of it, creates a vacuum between its rear end and the following car's nose.

Duct work The enclosures sealing heat exchangers, radiators, oil coolers, and so on, while forcing cool air to flow through each. Brake ducts direct cool air through hoses to cool rotors under racing conditions. Greater numbers of openings in the front of the air dam, grilles, etc., decrease the amount of downforce produced and increase drag. Teams not only control critical water-temperature and oil-temperature numbers, but can tailor handling by the addition or subtraction of tape on noses.

DYNO Short form for dynamometer, a machine used to measure an engine's horsepower and test and monitor its overall performance.

Economy run Driving slower to conserve fuel.

EIRI "Except in rare instances" A term describing NASCAR's ability to enforce its decisions when there may not be a specific rule or regulation to cover such a decision.

Engine displacement The volume within an engine's cylinders, expressed in cubic inches, that is swept by each piston as it makes one stroke downward, from top dead center (TDC) to bottom dead center (BDC). NASCAR rules only allow small block V8 engines with a minimum of 350 cubic-inch displacement (CID) and a maximum of 358 CID.

Equalize Cars in superspeedway races are required to run tires with both inner tubes and inner liners, which are actually small tires inside the standard tires. When the inner liner loses air pressure and that pressure becomes the same as that within the outer tire, the tire is said to have equalized and a vibration is created.

Factory A term designating the "Big Three" auto manufacturers, General Motors, Ford and Chrysler. The "factory days" refer to periods in the 1950s and '60s when the manufacturers actively and openly provided sponsorship money and technical support to some race teams.

FIA Fédération Internationale de l'Automobile, the governing body for most auto racing around the world.

Flagman The person standing on the tower above the start/finish line who controls the race with a series of flags.

Footprint The amount in square inches that each tire touches the earth. Larger footprints enhance tire grip to track. Four equal footprints with equally applied forces would promote great tire wear and vehicle handling.

Fresh rubber A new set of tires acquired during a pit stop.

Front clip The front-most part of the race car, starting with the firewall.

Front stretch The straight on a circle track between turns four and one. Also called "front straight" or "front chute," the start/finish line is usually there.

Gear ratio The number of teeth on a ring-gear divided into the number of teeth on a pinion-gear. Different size tracks use different gear ratios to obtain optimum performance for speed and fuel economy.

Get under Outbrake an opponent on the inside of a turn and make a pass.

Greasy See Slick.

Grenaded Destroyed an engine under racing conditions, usually in a dramatic show of smoke and fluids.

Groove The best route around a racetrack; also, the most efficient or quickest way around the track for a particular driver. The high groove takes a car closer to the outside wall for most of a lap. The low groove takes a car closer to the apron than the outside wall. Road racers use the term "line."

Handling A car's performance while racing, qualifying or practicing. How a car handles is determined by its tires, suspension geometry, aerodynamics and other factors.

Happy hour The final practice of a race weekend, usually late Saturday afternoon.

Headsock A fire-resistant head mask or balaclava.

Hole shot A drag racing term for beating an opponent off the starting line and winning a race despite having a slower elapsed time. Other racers use this term to describe a good start or restart.

Hooked up Term used to describe a car that is performing excellently because all parts are working well together.

Horsepower The estimated power needed to lift 33,000 pounds by one foot per minute – roughly equated with a horse's strength.

Independent A driver or team owner who does not have financial backing from a major sponsor and must make do with second-hand equipment such as parts and tires. The term, like the breed, is becoming rarer every year.

Infield The enclosed portion of a track, which includes team garages on most oval tracks. During race weekends, this area is usually filled with large transporters, merchandise trailers, and driver and fan motor homes.

Inner liner The tire within the tire. The tires used in some NASCAR racing have a second tire inside the main tire, which meets the race surface.

Inside groove or line On an oval track, this is the innermost racing line, which is usually separated from the infield by a distinctly flat surface called an apron. On road courses, the inside groove refers to the line closest to the curbs or walls forming the inner portion of turns.

Lap One time around a track. Also used as a verb when a driver passes a car and is a full lap ahead of (has "lapped") that opponent. A driver laps the field by overtaking every other car in the race.

Lapped traffic Cars that have dropped one or more laps behind the race leader after being passed by the lead driver and others on the lead lap.

Lift To raise or lift your foot off the gas pedal. Commonly used when drivers have to lift after an unsuccessful pass attempt to slow down and get back into the racing line.

Line See Groove.

Long pedal Commonly refers to a car's gas pedal because of the design. Also used to describe a brake pedal when brakes wear out because the driver has to push the pedal harder and further to slow down.

Loose A car that has more grip in the front than the rear end and tends to fishtail; a handling condition describing the tendency of a car's rear wheels to break away from the pavement, swinging its rear end toward the outside wall. Drivers often report whether the car is loose or tight so the crew can make adjustments.

Loose stuff Debris such as sand, pebbles or small pieces of rubber that tend to collect on a track's apron or near the outside wall.

Low drag set-up Adjusting a car's aerodynamic features to minimize drag, which also reduces downforce. This set-up achieves better performance on straightaways and reduced cornering ability. "Drag" is the amount of horsepower it takes to push the car through the air. At restrictor-plate races like Daytona and Talladega, you trade drag for downforce, so you have lower drag in order to have more downforce.

Marbles Rocks and debris that collect off the racing line. If a driver enters the marbles at an excessive speed, his car will lose grip and drive perilously into awaiting hazards. See Loose stuff.

Motor mounts Supports for the engine and transmission on a race car's frame, on which the motor sits in relation to the body of the car. NASCAR requires all motor mounts to be reinforced steel or aluminum, and adjustable mounts are not allowed. NASCAR teams strive to lower the motor mounts so that the car will have a lower center of gravity and handle better.

NASCAR Acronym for the National Association for Stock Car Auto Racing. Organization founded in December 1947 by

William (Bill) France Sr. and others, which sanctions races, sets rules and awards points toward championships for several types of stock cars: Nextel Cup, Craftsman Truck and Busch Grand National Series, among others.

Neutral A term for how a driver's car is handling; when a car is neither loose nor pushing (tight).

On the throttle A driver has the pedal to the metal.

Open-wheel Formula One and Indy-style race cars that are designed to have the suspension, wheels and tires exposed with no provision for fenders.

Outbrake A driver gains time and position on an opponent by applying the brakes later and deeper into a corner.

Outside groove The outside racing line. Sometimes a car will handle and perform better on the outside/inside line and a driver opts not to use the optimum groove.

Oval An oval-shaped track. Most NASCAR races are held on a track of this shape.

Oversteer When the front of a car has more grip than the rear. This is the same as a car being loose.

Parade lap The warm-up lap before a race. Drivers use this lap to warm up their engines and often zigzag to warm up tires.

Parking lot After a big crash that takes out a lot of cars, the track looks like a parking lot.

Penalty box Derived from ice hockey. NASCAR's way of penalizing drivers for infractions by holding them in the pits or behind the wall for a specified time during a race after a driver is caught doing something against the rules.

Pit stop An integral part of most racing series where drivers stop in pit row so their crews can change tires, refuel and make repairs or other adjustments.

Points race The overall competition to win the Drivers' or Manufacturers' championship at the end of the season.

Pole position The driver qualifying fastest is awarded the first starting position. This means the driver will start on the inside (relative to the first turn) of the first row.

Post-entry A team or driver who submits an entry blank for a race after the deadline for submission has passed. A post-entry receives no Nextel Cup points in NASCAR racing.

Provisional starting spot Special performance-based exemptions for drivers who do not initially qualify for a race. A position NASCAR holds open for certain drivers, such as past champions, who had trouble qualifying for the race. A driver awarded a provisional spot must start at the back of the starting grid.

Push The rear end of a car has more grip than the front. This condition makes a car harder to turn into a corner. Commonly known as "understeer."

Pushing Handling characteristics of a car where its front end tends to push or plow toward the outside wall in a corner.

Qualify During designated sessions, teams must meet established lap times to qualify for (or enter) a race based on a predetermined number of spots available.

Race rubber Race tires as opposed to qualifying tires.

Racer's tape Heavy-duty duct tape used to temporarily repair hanging body parts that might hinder aerodynamic features and decrease performance.

Rear roll center Located simply at the center of the track bar from the ground and center from the right to left mounting points. Roll centers are measured from the ground, but are relative to center of gravity. Higher roll centers exert less mechanical advantage, so lower spring rates can control roll or weight transfer.

Rear spoiler Two nonadjustable aluminum pieces attached side by side to equal a rail on the trunk of the car. Spoilers create downforce to improve the car's handling. NASCAR alters the size and angle now and then to create parity among manufacturers.

Reasonable suspicion, substance Both refer to NASCAR's drug-testing policy. Under the policy, if a NASCAR official is reasonably suspicious that a driver, crew member or another official is abusing drugs, the individual may be required to undergo testing. Substances include cocaine, heroin, PCP and other illegal drugs, as well as alcohol and prescription drugs while participating in an event.

Restrictor plate An aluminum plate with four holes in it that is placed under the carburetor to restrict air and fuel. That restriction keeps the cars from reaching speeds that NASCAR considers dangerous.

Right combination Catch-all phrase to describe why a car, team or driver has performed well or won a race. Included are engine horsepower; tire wear; correct weight distribution; and performance of the driver on the track or the crew on pit stops.

Road course A racetrack with multiple left- and right-hand turns. Generally refers to permanent, purpose-built racing facilities. Can also refer to temporary street courses built on big city streets, which were popularized in the 1980s. NASCAR's Nextel Cup series includes two road-racing venues.

Roll bars Large, sturdy bars designed to protect a driver if the car rolls over. Very functional in race cars but used more for style in production cars.

Roof flap A device made to keep the car from turning over. It works like an airplane flap and comes up when the car slides sideways or backward, to help slow down the car and keep it on the ground.

Running anywhere A car is handling so well, a driver can use any racing line (or drive anywhere). Sometimes, handling problems lead to a preferred line where the car handles better.

Running light A car is running with little fuel. Teams qualify with a light load to achieve maximum speed.

Sandbagging Allegedly failing to drive a car to its full potential in practice or qualifying, thus being able to provide a surprise for competitors during a race.

Saving the car/tires Driving a car somewhat moderately to conserve the car's mechanical parts and reduce tire wear. This allows a driver to be more aggressive during the all-important final laps.

Scrub The amount of force exerted on the tire footprint due to the different location of tire center or pivot and the actual pivot of the spindle.

Scrubbed tires The best kind of racing tires because they've had a few laps of wear to normalize the surface.

Scuff A tire that has been used at least once and is saved for further racing. A lap or two is enough to scuff it in.

Set-up The combination of settings for a car's engine, aerodynamic features and tires/wheels. Teams make continual adjustments to a car's set-up during pit stops based on driver input.

Shoot out Two or more drivers race to the end for victory.

Short track A speedway under a mile in distance.

Silly season Slang for the period that begins during the latter part of the season, when some teams announce driver, crew and/or sponsor changes.

Slick A track condition where, for a number of reasons, a car's tires do not properly adhere to the surface or get a good bite. A slick racetrack is not necessarily wet or slippery because of oil, water and so on.

Slingshot A maneuver in which a car following the leader in a draft suddenly steers around it, breaking the vacuum; this provides an extra burst of speed that allows the second car to take the lead. See Drafting.

Slip stream The cavity of low-pressure area created by a moving object. In racing, drivers use this slip stream to draft another vehicle.

Spoiler A metal strip that helps control airflow, downforce and drag. The front spoiler or air dam is underneath the car's front end near the axle; the rear spoiler is attached to the trunk lid. "Adding more spoiler" refers to increasing the rear spoiler's angle in relation to the rear window and generally aids a car's cornering ability. Less spoiler, decreasing its angle, aids straight-away speed.

Sponsor An individual or business establishment that financially supports a race driver, team, race or series of races in return for advertising and marketing benefits.

Stagger On ovals, teams may use a different size tire ("stagger") on the outside wheel to improve the car's handling ability. Also, the difference in size between the tires on the left and right sides of a car. Because of a tire's make-up, slight variations in circumference result. If the left-side tire is 87 inches, and the right-side tire is 88 inches, you have one inch of stagger.

Sticker(s) A new tire or tires. Term comes from the manufacturer's stick-on label denoting the type of tire, price and so on. Teams generally use sticker tires during qualifying, then use scrubbed tires in a race.

Stop-and-go penalty A penalty that requires a driver to stop at his team's pit for a timed penalty before reentering the race. This penalty can be assessed for anything from speeding in the pits to contact with an opponent.

Superspeedway A racetrack of a mile or more in distance. Road courses are included. Note: Racers refer to three types of oval tracks. Short tracks are under a mile; intermediate tracks are at least a mile, but under two miles; and speedways are two miles and longer.

Taped off Usually refers to applying racer's tape to the brake duct opening in full-bodied cars.

Tech Short for tech inspection, or technical inspection. Each car is submitted to tech inspection so sanctioning-body officials can confirm that all chassis and engine parts meet Series' guidelines. A "teched" car has passed inspections.

Telemetry Highly sophisticated electronics that transmit performance data from a car on the track back to team members.

Template A piece of aluminum that is placed on the cars to regulate the body sizes and diameters to make sure the body stays the way the manufacturer submitted it.

Tight Also known as "understeer." The car's front tires don't turn well through the turns because of traction loss. A driver must slow down entering and going through the turns to avoid having the car push all the way into the wall.

Tow-in The amount of distance the front tires are angled in toward the center of the car.

Track bar Connects the rear housing to the frame of the car and keeps it centered under the vehicle. It can be adjusted up and down to change the car's handling characteristics during pit stops.

Tri-oval The configuration of a racetrack that has a hump or fifth turn in addition to the standard four corners. Not to be confused with a triangle-shaped speedway, which has only three distinct corners.

Tuck under Drive closely enough behind an opponent's car to move into (or "tuck under") its draft.

Turbulence Rough air encountered by race car drivers.

200-mph tape Racer's tape, or duct tape, so strong it will hold a banged-up race car together long enough to finish a race.

Understeer When a car has more traction (or grip) in the rear than in the front.

Unlap A driver down one lap passes the leader to regain position on the lead lap.

Valance The panel that extends below the vehicle's front bumper. The relation of the bottom of the valance, or its ground clearance, affects the amount of front downforce the vehicle creates. Lowering the valance creates more front downforce. Also referred to as "front air dam."

War wagon Slang for the large metal cabinet on wheels that holds equipment in the driver's pit box during the race. Also called "pit wagon."

Warm-up lap The lap before a race starts. Drivers use this parade lap to warm up their engines and tires.

Weaving Zigzagging across the track to warm up and clean off tires, or to confuse an opponent while attempting a pass.

Wedge The cross-weight difference; that is, the amount of weight on the left rear and right front of the car.

Wind tunnel A structure used by race teams to determine the aerodynamic efficiency of their vehicles, consisting of a platform on which the vehicle is fixed and a giant fan used to create wind currents. Telemetry devices determine the airflow over the vehicle and its coefficient of drag and downforce.

Wrench Slang for racing mechanic.

Zigzag To move sharply back and forth on the track. Drivers often zigzag on warm-up laps to heat up their tires.

Photo Credits